High Schools on a Human Scale

Also by Thomas Toch

In the Name of Excellence

High Schools
on a
Human Scale

How Small Schools
Can Transform
American Education

Thomas Toch

Beacon Press, Boston

BEACON PRESS
25 Beacon Street
Boston, Massachusetts 02108-2892
www.beacon.org

Beacon Press books are published under the auspices of the
UNITARIAN UNIVERSALIST ASSOCIATION of CONGREGATIONS.

07 06 05 04 03   8 7 6 5 4 3 2 1

This book is printed on acid-free paper that meets the uncoated paper ANSI/NISO
specifications for permanence as revised in 1992.

Text design by Isaac Tobin
Composition by Wilsted & Taylor Publishing Services

Library of Congress Cataloging-in-Publication Data
Toch, Thomas.
  High schools on a human scale : how small schools can transform
American education / Thomas Toch.
    p. cm.
Includes bibliographical references.
  ISBN 080703245x (alk. paper)
  1. Small schools—United States—Case studies. 2. School size—United
States—Case studies. 3. Education, Secondary—United States—Case studies.
4. School improvement programs—United States—Case studies. I. Title.
LB3012.5.T63 2003
373.2'6—dc21   2002155245

For Ann, Matthew, and Caroline

Contents

Foreword

by Thomas Vander Ark

The prosperous, exurban Enumclaw school system in Washington State has a solid reputation and some of the best teachers and administrators that I've ever seen. But Enumclaw is also representative of a quiet crisis in American education: only about a third of the district's high school students—and a third of high school students nationally—receive the rigorous education they need for college, work, and productive citizenship in today's complex world. Another third of Enumclaw's students graduate seriously undereducated, says Art Jarvis, the district's reform-minded superintendent, and another third don't earn diplomas at all. High schools are respected, even cherished, institutions in American life. But the vast majority of the nation's high schools were designed for another time, and today they are far out of sync with the demands of our diverse republic and a global economy. Our high schools are obsolete.

Thomas Toch begins this book with an incisive analysis of the nation's high school crisis, explaining why large, comprehensive high schools no longer work. Then, in compelling, human terms, he presents a way out of the crisis. He takes us inside four schools and a school complex that collectively comprise a new vision of high schooling in America.

They are diverse schools—one is located in rural Minnesota and is run by a teacher cooperative, another occupies a former Navy warehouse in San Diego. But they share critical common characteristics: They are small, personal educational settings with a maximum of under a hundred students per grade, where the anonymity and incoherence of comprehensive high schools has given way to a powerful sense of community and a strong commitment to academic rigor.

The schools that Toch profiles are representative of a growing number of redesigned and new small high schools in the nation. In the past three years, my colleagues and I at the Bill & Melinda Gates Foundation have had the opportunity to visit dozens of small schools where over 90 percent of the students graduate and continue their education. Like the schools in this book, they engage all students in rigorous, relevant, and coherent courses of study that prepare students for college, work, and citizenship. The foundation is encouraging the spread of such schools through its grant-making out of a conviction that only by redesigning the American high school can we prepare students, particularly African American and Hispanic students, for today's demanding world.

The diversity of the schools is one of their most encouraging features. School reform is frequently a contentious, ideological, and partisan enterprise in America. Liberals fight with conservatives over reform strategies. Progressives clash with traditionalists. But the nascent new high school movement has transcended these long-standing battle lines. We have found the core characteristics of such schools—their small size, strong sense of community, autonomy, focus, high standards, adult advocacy for students, and parental choice—in Christian academies with traditional teaching strategies and we've found them in ultraprogressive schools. The new high school movement offers common ground to school reformers with widely varying political and pedagogical perspectives, making it not only a highly important national school reform priority, but also a politically feasible one.

A national system of new small high schools requires the creation of many new high schools and a "choice" system that permits students to select their schools and thus encourages schools to be different in interesting and meaningful ways. A system of such high schools also requires us to think differently about school system governance. Small, focused, and autonomous schools imply systems of diverse schools that educate all students to high levels. As a result, state and local school boards need to become managers of portfolios of schools; instead of operating schools, as they do now, boards need to ensure that all students have access to the variety of quality educational options supplied by many institutions and organizations.

Many of the nation's large, urban school systems have begun to address these needs, opening charter schools, for example, and initiating intra-district choice plans that permit students to attend high schools outside of their neighborhoods. But as Enumclaw suggests, the troubles with comprehensive high schools are not confined to the inner cities. More than five thousand students drop out of American high schools every school day, in middle-class suburbs, rural towns, major urban centers, and everywhere in between.

It may take 10,000 new schools to address the problem. And it may take $10 billion in public and private funding to fix the high schools we have and to create the new ones we need. Since 2000 the Bill & Melinda Gates Foundation has pledged $600 million to the task. With the foundation's help, a dozen organizations are building networks of new small, personalized high schools. New schools are particularly important for underserved students, increasing their educational options, reducing enrollments in overcrowded schools, and leveraging change in other existing schools through competition for students.

Improving American high school education, particularly the graduation rates of African-American and Hispanic students (and, subsequently, their college completion rates), is the focus of the foundation's work in education. We salute and support those who are leading this fight—teachers who never give up on students, principals who hold fast to a vision of a great school for poor children, superintendents who build a sense of community, educational entrepreneurs, community organizations fighting for families, university deans who roll up their sleeves in schools, mayors with a visions of great cities, governors who know that education equals jobs. And we salute students—especially those who grow up in America in poverty and those who come to this country for a better life—who, in the face of great odds, persevere to gain an education.

The schools portrayed in this book represent a beginning, a pathway. They are examples of what is possible. The educators at the schools are people of courage and vision, people who daily pursue justice in tough places.

Introduction

The basic blueprint of the nation's high schools hasn't changed significantly since the rise of the "comprehensive" high school nearly a century ago. And the nation's high school students—and the nation itself—are paying a heavy price as a result. This book is a response to this crisis in American education. It is about a new, more successful model of secondary schooling—one that has begun to take shape around the country.

The problem is that comprehensive high schools were created to do something quite different from what we want, and need, high schools to do today.

Prior to the early 1900s and the emergence of the comprehensive model, only a fraction of the nation's students—

about 10 percent—had stayed in school long enough to get to high school, and they studied traditional academic subjects, like history and chemistry and English literature. Serving a small elite, they educated the professionals and managers who ran the country and its major institutions.

But at the beginning of the twentieth century educators faced an influx of new students, often from other countries, who were thought to be ill-equipped to study high school–level academics. Leaders of the Progressive movement such as John Dewey pushed to extend the high school curriculum beyond traditional academic subjects and to include more students in higher grades, on the grounds that doing so would help make American life and culture more democratic. And a new and influential "child-centered" theory of learning encouraged schools to build their curricula around their students' daily lives.

Public educators' priorities shifted quickly. The National Education Association, the leading public education organization of the day, established a Commission on the Reorganization of Secondary Education. In a widely publicized 1918 report entitled the "Cardinal Principles of Secondary Education," the commission declared that the "main objectives" of secondary education should be "1. Health. 2. Command of fundamental processes [literacy skills]. 3. Worthy home-membership. 4. Vocation. 5. Citizenship. 6. Worthy use of leisure. 7. Ethical character."

Before long, high schools were adding a wide range of

vocational and other nonacademic subjects to their traditional offerings. Suddenly the best high school was a comprehensive high school, one that taught a wide range of students many different things, rather than a school that taught academics to everyone. Studies had turned up only 40 different high school courses in the years before the publication of the Cardinal Principles. But twenty years after the report's publication there were 274 subjects taught in the nation's high schools and only 59 of them involved traditional academic disciplines. Half of the nation's students were attending high school.

The rapid expansion of the high school curriculum beyond its traditional academic boundaries led to the establishment of distinct curriculum paths into which educators placed students based on the students' perceived "needs," a practice later known as "tracking."

This utilitarian system of secondary education served the purposes of the nation's industrial economy. It taught traditional academic disciplines to lawyers, accountants, and other professions and to the managerial class in industry. And it taught less demanding, more practical subjects to those headed into mills and onto assembly lines, where the work simply didn't require very much advanced "book learning." High schools essentially served as sorting machines, preparing students very differently for very different roles in the workforce.

The system was thought to be both efficient and egalitarian. It represented a deliberate attempt by educators to apply the industrial principles of mass production to the task of providing secondary schooling on a mass scale. Students were placed onto different educational assembly lines according to the type of product they were to become.

Eventually, a former Harvard University president would use his national platform to extol the virtues of the comprehensive high school. In a highly influential 1959 book, *The American High School Today,* James B. Conant argued that only large, comprehensive schools could achieve the economies of scale necessary to supply students with the range of courses required by their diverse educational needs. Bigger, richer, more efficient schools could do more than multiple smaller schools with smaller budgets. He further argued that by tending to students' different needs "under one roof" comprehensive high schools were an important source of the "democratic spirit" in public education, a stance shared by many educators in subsequent years as they sought to bring disadvantaged and minority students into the educational mainstream in the wake of the civil rights movement.

Conant's endorsement intensified educators' loyalty to the concept of the comprehensive high school, and his declaration that small schools represented "one of the serious obstacles to good secondary education throughout most of the United States" quickened a nascent movement to consolidate the nation's schools and school systems. "Small" to

Conant meant schools with a senior class of under one hundred students. His critique was based in some fact: many tiny, isolated schoolhouses dotted the educational landscape, lacking both resources and educational expertise. But Conant's rhetoric led educators to think in terms of vastly larger secondary schools. And today 60 percent of American ninth through twelfth graders attend high schools of at least one thousand students.

But the nation has entered a new era that has put new demands on high schools—demands that require replacing the comprehensive high school with something very different. One set of demands are economic. Sorting students into curriculum tracks with widely varying standards sufficed in an industrial era when a majority of jobs required workers to use their hands rather than their heads and paid them well for doing so. But in today's "knowledge-based" economy, where decent-paying jobs require brains rather than brawn, only students who are taught to use their minds well have a shot at a middle-class lifestyle or more. No longer is it enough for high schools to educate only the best and brightest to high levels.

The new economy requires a new and different priority: that nearly every student be educated well enough to enter college, a notion that the founders of the comprehensive high school simply didn't contemplate.

The stakes are high. The U.S. Department of Commerce

reports that students with a bachelor's degree earned 61 percent more than students with only a high school diploma in 2000, compared to a wage gap of only 27 percent a decade earlier. Such numbers suggest that the "democratic spirit" in education, invoked by Dewey and Conant, today means providing students from a wide range of backgrounds with the same demanding high school education that in the past has been reserved for the gifted and the privileged.

Modern democratic life also demands more of high schools. Effective citizenship in today's complex world requires a level of knowledge—about science, global politics, and a host of other subjects—that in the past only a small elite possessed.

American high schools have, of course, sought to expand their academic mandate in recent decades. By traditional yardsticks, they are arguably as successful as they've ever been. When one includes students earning Graduate Equivalent Diplomas, a higher percentage of students now graduate from high school than at any other time in the nation's history.

But there are fundamental flaws in the comprehensive high schools that make it impossible for them to achieve today's unprecedented goal of delivering a rigorous academic education to a majority of students.

Because they try to teach so many different subjects to students who they believe to have sharply differing educational priorities, comprehensive high schools are highly fragmented institutions. Rarely do students, parents, teachers, and administrators share a sense of what their schools' priorities should be. There is an absence of "focus" in the schools' curricula and culture.

Rarely, as a result, are comprehensive high schools able to concentrate their energies and their resources in ways that are likely to produce the strongest results. And rarely are they able to engender a strong sense of community—a strong sense of connectedness—among students, teachers, and parents. The community spirit of Friday night football games rarely carries over to the daily life of comprehensive high schools. To the contrary, comprehensive high schools tend to be intensely impersonal places, where strong, sustained relationships among teachers and between students and teachers are rare.

The result, in many comprehensive high schools, is a high level of alienation and apathy among students and teachers. The anonymity that pervades many public high schools saps students' motivation to learn and teachers' motivation to teach. In many classes, students merely go through the motions, united with equally disaffected teachers in what the educator Theodore Sizer trenchantly described as a "conspiracy of the least"—an unwritten, unspoken pledge to put as little energy as possible into their work. And these classroom compromises take a huge toll on public high schools' productivity.

They also stand as a tremendous barrier to the nation's

goal of extending public education's academic reach. Attempts to bolster academic instruction aren't likely to amount to much if students aren't motivated to learn. And alienated educators have scant incentive to abandon the long-held view in public education that a majority of students are incapable of doing demanding academic work. By believing that many students can't handle higher-level academics, educators absolve themselves of the responsibility of teaching such material to them. It's much easier to teach students how to use cash registers in a "retail merchandising" course than it is to try to teach them physics, chemistry, or biology.

The comprehensive high school model also diminishes student learning in another way. The thick course catalogues in comprehensive high schools require daily schedules so complex that they lock school administrators into using traditional forty-five-minute classes. But in so doing they typically deny teachers both the opportunity to design interdisciplinary courses with others on the faculty and the opportunity to have students apply what they've learned through projects outside of schools. The result: many students are less motivated to learn because they don't grasp the relevance of what they are studying.

The large size of many comprehensive high schools— enrollments of three or four thousand students aren't uncommon in major cities—only makes these problems worse. Big schools are bureaucratic places. Roles and relationships are defined largely by rules and regulations. That erodes teachers' stake in their schools' success. The faculties of many high schools are so large that it's hard for them even to discuss school policies together.

Students typically work much harder in the classroom when they sense their teachers and other adults in their schools value them. But in large schools teachers struggle merely to learn their students' names. And the physical atmosphere in many sprawling comprehensive high schools is less than welcoming. Many are drab, cinderblock fortresses, with metal detectors, elaborate pass systems, and burly administrators continuously patrolling hallways and grounds, linked by gasping walkie-talkies. For many students, large comprehensive high schools are joyless, uninspiring places.

And though Conant declared that comprehensive high schools would foster a "democratic spirit," it is disadvantaged and minority students who have paid the highest price for the failings of comprehensive secondary schools. They have arrived at the nation's high schools needing the most academic enrichment and the most adult advocacy and routinely have received the least.

Nor have sprawling high schools proved to be as efficient as Conant predicted. In the four decades since the publication of *The American High School Today* many state legislators and others in charge of public education's purse strings have been among the strongest advocates of Conant's compre-

9

hensive high school, believing that big schools would save taxpayers money. But new research by faculty at New York University has found that small high schools (those with fewer than 400 students) spend on average only about 5 percent more per student than large schools (those with more than 2,000 students), and they found that small schools spend slightly less than large schools per graduate because the large schools have a higher percentage of students who don't earn diplomas.

In the end, big high schools don't even deliver very well on the basic promise of a richer curriculum. Rather than provide higher level courses in foreign languages, math, and other core subjects, many large high schools squander their additional resources on introductory courses in peripheral subjects such as auto mechanics and business.

For a majority of students, particularly African American and Hispanic students and those from disadvantaged families, a large, comprehensive high school is an educational dead end, where low expectations and tracking swell enrollments in courses like "introduction to consumer math" instead of geometry, algebra, and trigonometry.

James Conant was well intentioned when he wrote *The American High School Today*. But he was wrong.

Respected reformers who studied high schools in the early 1980s had come to much the same conclusion. Ernest Boyer, president of the Carnegie Foundation for the Advancement of Teaching, pointed in *High School: A Report on Secondary Education in America* to the size and impersonality of comprehensive high schools as a primary source of the alienation and apathy he found among students and teachers. So did University of Washington professor John Goodlad in *A Place Called School* and Theodore Sizer, a former dean of the Harvard Graduate School of Education, in *Horace's Compromise*, a study of life in comprehensive high schools. They recommended that comprehensive high schools be reshaped into smaller educational settings.

A few educators began to act on that belief, including Anthony Alvarado, the superintendent of District 4 in New York City. Troubled by the poor performance of his East Harlem students, Alvarado shut down three sprawling comprehensive junior high schools and replaced them with upward of fifteen small, autonomous educational programs that he had encouraged District 4's strongest teachers to create. And then he introduced market competition into his reform equation, *requiring* students to choose from among the new programs—and thus forcing the programs to compete for students. Alvarado's returns were fabulous: By the end of the 1980s District 4's student achievement had risen from thirty-second among New York City's thirty-two local school systems to sixteenth.

One of the teachers that Alvarado had empowered was Deborah Meier, an elementary school teacher who earned a national reputation and a MacArthur Foundation "genius" award for founding the two-hundred-student Central Park East Secondary School for Alvarado. Her work would spread to other parts of New York City and beyond. And the small high schools movement also got a lift from a growing number of magnet programs in large urban high schools.

But the recommendations on school size by the 1980s reformers never received the attention they deserved. The reports by Boyer, Sizer, Goodlad, and others spawned an immense amount of school reform. But the plight of the comprehensive high school was pushed to the side in favor of other priorities.

Then in 2000 the Bill & Melinda Gates Foundation launched a five-year initiative to replace the comprehensive high school with a very different institution, one designed to educate many more students to a much higher level, as today's economy demands. In identifying the key qualities of such a school, the foundation's education staff interviewed hundreds of leading educators, traveled to scores of high-performing high schools, and studied a wide range of research on the nation's high schools.

The foundation discovered, as Boyer, Sizer, Goodlad, and others had before them, that high schools are more likely to be successful when they are small and personalized—when they have no more than four hundred students and stress long-term relationships between students and teachers, individualized attention, extra help for struggling students, and an adult advocate for every student. Smaller schools encourage stronger bonds between students and teachers and generate a level of genuine caring and mutual obligation between them that's found far less frequently in comprehensive high schools.

Students and teachers, as a result, tend to work harder on each other's behalf. Student and teacher attendance and student involvement in extracurricular activities are higher in smaller high schools. Teacher turnover and disciplinary problems are lower. So are dropout rates. There's less tracking in smaller schools. And a wide range of studies reveal that average student achievement is as high as and often higher than that in large schools, particularly among students from impoverished backgrounds.

But other things also contribute to such results.

The best schools have a clear sense of what they hope to achieve with their students. They are "focused." Their curricula, their teaching strategies, the way they organize their school day, even, in many instances, the design of their buildings, are aligned with their educational aims. Every productive school has a core set of educational beliefs that shapes what its educators do and how they do it.

Successful schools also have high academic expectations for every student. That is their defining characteristic. They reject the tradition in public education of tracking large percentages of students into largely nonacademic courses. They reject the notion of "comprehensiveness" in high schools. They want to prepare every student for post-secondary success.

In the classroom they stretch students' minds, often by teaching fewer topics in greater depth, by stressing student projects and presentations, and by having students apply what they've learned through community-based intern-ships. They stress student competence, not curriculum coverage.

They are organized to make students active learners—inquiring, questioning, independent-minded individuals, not passive receptacles of received wisdom. Students in such schools routinely present their work to live audiences (teachers, parents, peers, college professors, and other out-siders), and they must demonstrate a capacity to use knowl-edge in different ways. They use technology as a tool to delve deeper into the subjects they study.

Teachers play a different role in these schools than they do in traditional high schools. Instead of lecturing students, they help students teach themselves, a task that's akin to coaching.

The social climate in high-achieving high schools stresses respect and responsibility. Students and teachers study and work in the schools by choice. And the schools supply teachers with the time and the resources they need to collaborate as professionals. They promote adult learning as well as student learning. And they signal to teachers and principals that they're far more than mere cogs in a bureaucratic wheel by giving them authority over budgets, curriculum, and staffing.

The following chapters take readers inside schools with many of these characteristics of educational excellence. The Gates Foundation discovered the schools as it searched for solutions to the crisis in the comprehensive high school, and it is helping several of them replicate their models in other places.

I joined the Gates project to tell the schools' stories. I had known several of them by reputation, through my work as an education writer. But under the foundation's auspices I set out to learn the inspirations of the schools' innovations, the challenges of sustaining such innovations in public school systems, and the prospects for replicating the experiments elsewhere and on a wide scale.

The schools are located in rural, urban, and suburban communities, they enroll students from a wide range of family backgrounds, and they operate on the same amount of funding per pupil as traditional high schools in their locales. Several have embraced progressive teaching strategies (now with the aim of helping disadvantaged students achieve at the same high levels thought to be beyond their reach by many who claimed to be progressives in the past).

But I could have profiled any number of schools with a wide range of teaching strategies and curriculum priorities, such as 420-student Noble Street Charter High School in Chicago, where students wear uniforms and study a traditional curriculum, or Rehoboth Christian School in New Mexico. The reform-minded high schools that the schools in this book represent are as diverse as they are innovative.

The Julia Richman Education Complex is a block-square "multiplex" on Manhattan's Upper East Side, a school that was long an urban failure but one that has been transformed into a federation of six separate and successful schools under a single roof.

At Urban Academy in the Julia Richman complex, a school serving many students who have failed at other New York City public high schools, teachers' traditional work as classroom lecturers has been abandoned in favor of a teaching methodology that puts students in leading roles in the classroom. And instead of taking traditional standardized graduation tests students must complete a series of long-term projects that culminate in public presentations.

The Metropolitan Regional Career and Technical Center in Providence, Rhode Island, known as The Met, encourages project-based learning and strong student-adult relationships by replacing traditional courses with a series of student internships in the Providence area.

At Gary and Jerri-Ann Jacobs High Tech High, a San Diego

charter school housed in a renovated Navy warehouse, students use technology to learn geometry, biology, and other core subjects through independent and group projects.

The Minnesota New Country School is a public charter school in a rural hamlet in southern Minnesota, a school that is run by the nation's first for-profit teacher cooperative.

The schools do not each have every element of high-performing high schools in place. They are works in progress. But collectively they reflect the potential for change in secondary education. They are examples of what can be done where vision and leadership are present together. They suggest that it is indeed possible to reinvent the American high school.

I **Re: Building**

Julia Richman Education Complex, New York City

To grasp the magnitude of Julia Richman's transformation over the past decade, talk to John Broderick, the school's veteran engineer.

Richman had opened as a public girls' high school back in the 1920s, a five-story, red-brick structure stretching from Sixty-seventh to Sixty-eighth Streets on Manhattan's Upper East Side. With classrooms for twenty-two hundred students, two gymnasiums, a swimming pool, a beautiful theater, maple floors, and brass doorknobs inscribed with the words, "Public School, City of New York," the school was a source of great civic pride. Its first students studied "commercial skills" such as typing and stenography. And then Greek and Latin and other advanced subjects entered the school's curriculum and Julia Richman became one of New York City's most prestigious secondary schools.

But by the early 1990s there were few traces of its proud past. Buffeted by a changing student population, sharp staffing cuts, and other forces, the enormous and by then coeducational school had degenerated into a cauldron of violence. Students tore out water fountains, destroyed bathrooms, and smashed windows, Broderick recalls. Graffiti covered the school's hallways. Metal cages were constructed in the vice-principal's office to separate belligerent students. Local cops labeled the school Julia Rikers, after New York City's notorious Riker's Island jail. It was, says Broderick, "utter, utter chaos." Not surprisingly, the inscription by philosopher Francis Bacon over the school's front door, "Knowledge Is Power," was lost on everyone: the school's graduation rate was 37 percent.

Today, though, Julia Richman is again a very different place. In Broderick's fervent words, "It has turned around 500 percent." The disciplinary cages are gone, as are the metal detectors that guarded the school's entrances. The school is bright, clean, and safe; fights are rare. Attendance is up. Dropout rates are down substantially. And greater numbers of graduates are going to college.

What produced this educational reformation at a time when the nation is lamenting the plight of its urban public high schools? A big part of the answer can be found in the names on the simple, two-foot by three-foot banners that hang largely unnoticed along the school's main corridor: Urban Academy, Vanguard, Manhattan International, Talent Unlimited, P226M, Ella Baker—the names of the separate schools that share what is now known as the Julia Richman Education Complex.

Like the other schools in this book—The Met in Providence, New Country in Henderson, Minnesota, and High Tech High in San Diego—Julia Richman has abandoned the American tradition of the "big high school" in favor of greatly scaled-down educational settings that engender a far stronger sense of community, where students care because they feel cared about.

Some small schools, including New Country, The Met, and High Tech High, are new schools in new or nonschool buildings. But the high cost of real estate in New York City (and many other urban centers), together with the city school system's already vast investment in bricks and mortar, make it financially unfeasible to abandon existing buildings like Julia Richman, even if they are big, prisonlike places.

Many urban educators have sought to address the unwieldiness and weaknesses of their large high schools by subdividing them into "houses," each with several hundred students and a team of teachers who work with the students throughout the students' high school careers.

That's a step in the right direction. But merely cleaving enormous urban high schools into smaller units is rarely enough to counter such schools' intensely impersonal environments and the apathy and alienation that they engender among students and teachers. Too often houses fail to establish organizational personalities that students and teachers can identify with, and the indifferent bureaucracy of the larger school continues to define life within houses.

New York City adopted a more radical—and more productive—strategy at Julia Richman. The city began to empty the building of students and staff beginning in the early 1990s and then introduced half a dozen new schools of no more than three hundred students, each with its own leadership, and each responsible for its own staffing, curriculum, and budgets.

Deborah Meier, the founder of Central Park East Secondary School, the small, nationally acclaimed high school in East Harlem, was the source of the Julia Richman concept. Convinced that New York's vast comprehensive high schools were organizationally bankrupt, she and others from the Coalition of Essential Schools, a national school reform network, in 1992 sought the permission of the New York City Board of Education to restructure one of the city's worst high schools. The board granted the request and gave Meier and her colleagues Julia Richman, which had been on New York State's list of failing schools for more than a decade.

The rechristened Julia Richman Education Complex stopped taking new ninth graders after the 1992–93 school year and by the summer of 1996 the last of the school's "old" students had graduated.

The coalition, meanwhile, moved new small schools into Julia Richman as space became available. The first were Vanguard High School, a school that takes primarily low-achieving students, and Manhattan International, serving recent immigrants who lack a strong grasp of English. At the same time, a performing-arts program within Julia Richman known as Talent Unlimited became an autonomous school within the new complex. Urban Academy Laboratory High School, a 120-student school for teenagers who have been unsuccessful in other city high schools, moved in shortly afterward.

The results have been outstanding, to the pleasant surprise of parents, the city's education leaders, and many others. The dropout rate at Vanguard, the Julia Richman school with the most challenging students, is only 4 percent (compared to 20 percent citywide) and Manhattan International and Urban Academy report that over 90 percent of their students go to college after graduation.

But remaking Julia Richman into an education "multiplex" was not simple. And ensuring that so many separate schools continue to work together effectively under a single roof has proven no less challenging. Indeed, if the creators of the Richman complex hadn't taken many steps along the way to preserve the independence of its individual schools without sacrificing the governability of the vast building, Richman wouldn't be the success it is today.

Early on, Meier and her colleagues resolved to not try to start half a dozen new schools in Richman. To open the educational complex with every school in the building in the throes of start-up would likely be disastrous, they reasoned. Instead, several of Richman's new high schools were "hothoused" in other locations around New York for a year, giving them time to work out the bugs in their school designs and time to establish distinct educational identities before moving to the Richman campus. As Herb Mack, codirector of Urban Academy and a Richman founder, puts it: "We wanted to make sure that the schools had a reason for being other than just being small." Hot-housing the schools also ensured that there would be no existing math, history, and other department heads to challenge the autonomy of the nascent schools—a problem for many high schools that merely subdivide themselves into houses.

Urban Academy played a key role in helping to establish the fledgling schools at Richman. It had been a highly successful Manhattan school for a decade and was moved into Richman as part of the school's overhaul to serve as an "anchor" institution within the building. Like Richman's other hot-housed schools, Urban was able to bring its stu-

dents to Richman under New York City's school choice program, which permits many students to select schools outside of their neighborhoods.

Urban's stature helped Richman's new high schools sur-
vive a troubled two-year coexistence with the students and
teachers they were replacing in the building. The transition
generated friction between the school's old and new staffs,
and it hurt the students in the high school that was being
phased out. "The 700–800 exiting kids were demoralized
and largely abandoned," says Ann Cook, who runs Urban
Acad-emy with Mack and who helped create the Richman
complex. "The existing staff were angry and suspicious.
'Now you are fixing the place,' they would say when they
saw workers doing renovations. It was horrible." Urban's
leaders helped to diffuse the hostility. But in retrospect they
concluded that it would have been better to move the new
schools into the building only after it had been vacated
completely.

Once the new schools arrived at the Richman complex,
Mack, Cook, and their colleagues went to great lengths to
preserve the schools' separateness—believing that creating
a strong sense of community within each of the new small
schools was the best way to forge the close, respectful relationships between students and teachers that motivate students to care about their school work.

Students had to apply to each school in the complex separately. And the majority of the students in the complex's schools attended them by choice—as a result of the city's choice plan—and were thus, Meier and the others reasoned, more likely to identify with the schools and to work harder as a result. In contrast, the majority of Richman's previous students were assigned to the school, many of them after being rejected by other New York City high schools.

The schools in the Richman complex are also physically distinct. Though as many as three of them share some floors of the building, there are no common hallways and the swinging double doors that connect the schools might as well be cinderblock walls; students and teachers simply don't go into other schools' space—a fact that has required a lot of instructional gerrymandering, including the moving of a chemistry lab to Manhattan International's wing of the building so that its students didn't have to enter Vanguard's area to go to class.

Even bathrooms, part of the discipline problem in many high schools, are part of the solution at Richman. To ensure that there aren't any public spaces where students and teachers aren't known to each other, every bathroom in the building has been located within the boundaries of schools and are off-limits to students from other schools in the building—conditions that have required students and teachers at Urban to use the same bathrooms. There are six schools in six different locations on six different schedules at Richman. They share a recital hall, art gallery, gym, pool, weight room, pottery and dance studios, cafeteria, library, an auditorium, a small theater, and a student health clinic run by nearby Mt. Sinai Hospital. The only places they are permitted to use at the same time are the cafeteria and the library.

In carving out distinct boundaries within the building and giving the schools authority over their staffing, budgets, and teaching strategies, Richman's organizers sought to give teachers a significant stake in their students' success. "Houses don't work," says Cook, "because you need autonomy for teachers for them to feel truly responsible for kids and houses don't create enough autonomy. You can't go halfway. If teachers don't feel responsible they don't invest themselves."

Richman's tightly knit schools, meanwhile, have engendered a sense of belonging among the school's students that rarely exists in large urban high schools. In the words of Urban Academy's Mack, a forty-year veteran of the Chicago and New York school systems, Richman's schools "give kids a home." Urban's atmosphere is best described as relaxed; there's little trace of the coldness and sense of unease that pervade many traditional urban public high schools. During breaks between classes Urban students hang out in groups in stuffed chairs and old sofas in the hallway of the school's second-floor "campus." As I sat speaking with Urban faculty members during a recent visit, several students dropped over and asked the teachers questions. They sought out teachers with no less casualness in Urban's faculty office, a large, open space with desks pushed up against each other, as in a newsroom.

"How many teachers did you know well at Midwood?" I asked Aneliese Ranzoni, a senior at Urban who had transferred from Midwood High School in Brooklyn, where there were thirty-seven hundred students.

"Know well?"

"Well."

"None."

"How about here?"

"All the ones I have, and also the ones I don't have."

The result, says Rona Armillas, a former assistant principal at Manhattan International, is "a different type of negotiation" between students and teachers in the Richman complex. "In most high schools you approach kids as an authority figure," Armillas says. "It's a power play. And it usually doesn't work. There's no growth in students' maturity. At Richman, you know the kid and his style and there's mutual respect. Things don't escalate." As Urban science teacher Terri Grosso puts it, "It's not us versus them here."

Security takes on a very different meaning in such an atmosphere. Rather than a system that treats students anonymously and resorts to using metal detectors and surveillance cameras, Richman's schools have been largely able to police themselves. Because of the schools' small size and Richman's complex wide policy of having students stay out of other schools' space, students and teachers know who belongs in their part of the building and who doesn't, and that becomes Richman's most important source of security. Students, in fact, are just as likely as teachers to ask "outsiders" for identification or to report them to Richman's half dozen security guards.

Richman of course isn't completely free of disciple problems, but serious infractions like fighting, say students such as Josme Mark, a senior from Haiti via Brooklyn, are very rare. That's certainly the sense one gets at the complex's front entrance, where a mild-mannered guard with a smile and a sign-in sheet has replaced metal detectors.

It's hard to overstate the care with which Richman's leaders have tended to the building's social equilibrium. To discourage interschool rivalries even as they promote schools' autonomy, for example, they have sought to blend students from the sundry Richman schools in carefully chosen settings. In addition to student councils in each school, there's a buildingwide student government. There are buildingwide college fairs. Students represent Richman rather than their individual schools in New York City's Public School Athletic League. And Richman's athletic director has begun commingling students from the different high schools on intramural basketball teams.

28

Yet a recent event at Richman reveals both the value of the building's policy of strict autonomy among its schools and the fragile nature of the social fabric in urban high schools. Mack had given the Richman girls' and boys' basketball teams each a classroom in Urban for prepractice study halls. Urban students are so trusting of one another that they routinely leave expensive jackets lying around in the student lounge. But as soon as the buildingwide basketball teams started coming into Urban, the clothing began to disappear. The basketball players brought friends from other Richman schools with them to the Urban study halls who simply didn't share the same sense of community as Urban's students. When Mack subsequently moved the study halls to the Richman theater, the theft at Urban subsided.

To protect the independence of the new Richman schools Meier and the others resolved that the complex wouldn't have a principal, only a "building manager"—Urban co-director Herb Mack.

To watch the veteran educator work the seventy-nine-year-old building it would be easy to think he were a traditional public school principal. When I caught up with him at 7:15 A.M. one morning he was speeding through Richman checking that its many doors were locked, a knot of keys bouncing up and down on his hip. He greeted the guards at the building's two student entrances. And then he bolted outside with a sheaf of reserved-for-staff flyers that he placed under the windshield wipers of cars parked on the school's block that didn't display school system parking permits. Back in the building he noticed that the day's newspapers weren't at the front entrance. "They've been taken again, we've got to find out who's doing it," he declared, striding toward a security guard to report the matter. By 7:45 he was welcoming students who had begun entering the building. And then he suddenly found himself sorting out a disagreement between Broderick's staff and security guards over a broken elevator.

But by 8:15 Mack had changed roles. He was back at his desk in Urban Academy, talking as the school's codirector to a student about a course she needed to complete her semester's schedule. And shortly afterward he headed down the hall to the first of the three social studies courses he teaches at Urban.

Mack's work as Richman's building manager also differs from that of traditional principals in other significant ways. Mack, who was named to his buildingwide role by the New York City superintendent for alternative high schools, has no authority over the budgets, staffing, or instruction at Richman's various schools, other than at Urban. And schoolwide policies are made by a "building council" that consists of the directors of Richman's schools and the heads of other programs now housed in the building: First Steps, a child care center; the health clinic; and a teacher training center. The council convenes once a week for a couple of hours to discuss everything from fire drills to food quality. It also gathers several times a year at the home of the director of one of Richman's schools for breakfast or lunch and a half-day's discussion. Mack leads the meetings, but he doesn't dictate their outcomes.

Early on, the council, then representing Richman's four high schools, decided to bring in an elementary program—the three-hundred-student pre-K through eighth Ella Baker Elementary School—and another for disabled students—P226M, serving several dozen autistic students—as a way of further tempering the adolescent environment in Richman. The strategy has paid substantial dividends: older students are more careful about what they say and do when younger children are present, and the presence of Ella Baker and P226M within Richman give the building's high school students ready opportunities to be tutors and teachers aides, responsible roles that they are encouraged to play. Notably, the bank of monitors that security guards at the old Richman watched twenty-four hours a day in a windowless second-floor office has been boxed off with plywood in what is now an Ella Baker counseling office.

The council reshaped Vanguard's boundaries when it realized that its original "traffic" plan had required Talent Unlimited students to go through Vanguard on their way to and from Richman's cafeteria. The result: the hallway between Talent Unlimited and the cafeteria was turned into "public" space, housing the complex's pottery and dance studios, home economics center, and distance-learning laboratory, which the building council constructed with city council funding.

And because many high school students in the building were parents, the council used school system funding to turn Richman's old guidance suites into the First Steps infant-toddler child care center, complete with an observation room and a one-way mirror for students in the building's child-development classes.

The council is tough-minded when it comes to Richman's public spaces. In the early days of the complex Talent Unlimited wanted control of a small auditorium where its choruses had practiced under the old Richman regime when it was semiautonomous. The council said, "No," and worked out a solution that Talent Unlimited could live with. The auditorium would be shared and scheduled through Mack, as is every public space in the building. But the council would buy Talent Unlimited risers that would permit the school's chorus to practice in one of its own classrooms.

When I was at Richman the building's guards were troubled by the substantial number of delivery people wandering the building. They expressed their unhappiness to the council's security subcommittee and by the next morning the council had taken action. "Delivery of food to staff and students has been a headache," Mack declared in a memo to the building's staff and students. As a result, he announced, "Any deliveries that arrive without the recipient's name and room number written on the back of the package will be sent back to the restaurant." Within a week the problem was solved.

But unless the welfare of Richman as a whole is at stake the council lets schools set policies individually. When the New York City Police Department wanted to ban "do rag" headwear in the city's schools as a way of discouraging gangs, the four Richman high schools responded independently. Manhattan International, Vanguard, and Talent Unlimited went along with the police request. But Urban, after a student-faculty meeting where dew rags were adjudged to have no gang overtones at the school, resolved to continue to let its students wear the apparel. Richman's other three high schools respected Urban's stance.

Though conventional thinking about small schools would suggest otherwise, the Richman multiplex hasn't been expensive to operate. Skeptics of small schools frequently contend that they must be less efficient than big schools because they can't spread costs over as many students. But the Richman complex in many instances has been more efficient than the large school it replaced. Julia Richman High School, for example, needed six extra security guards just to operate its metal detectors. Richman's

33

council has streamlined buildingwide staffing, in one instance reducing the number of elevator operators on the building's payroll to one per elevator, so that there wasn't an off-duty operator on the payroll every day. Schools in the Richman complex have required fewer counselors because teachers and administrators know students well. And because Richman's schools are small and thus more manageable, Mack and other administrators have time to teach. That has permitted the schools to focus more of their resources on their classrooms. Eighty-seven percent of the staff in Richman's high schools teach students, for example, compared to 81 percent in New York City's high schools generally.

The cost savings of these steps have been borne out by Norm Fruchter and his colleagues at New York University's Graduate School of Education. They recently examined the finances of large and small high schools nationwide and found that the efficiencies of large high schools are largely offset by fewer nonteaching staff and other savings in small schools. Small schools are only about 5 percent more expensive than large ones, they concluded. And when Fruchter and his associates considered the price tag of high schools from a new perspective—the cost per graduate—the efficiency debate tilted in favor of small high schools. Because dropout rates are higher in large high schools, Fruchter found, the cost of educating each graduate averaged

$49,578, compared to $49,554 in small high schools, where more students stay through graduation.

Richman's schools also work together to stretch their resources. Several of them have sought to concentrate their course offerings out of a desire to teach fewer subjects in greater depth. But by pooling their resources under the auspices of the building council, they have been able to hire shared staff in art, dance, and other subjects that they want to teach but wouldn't have been able to staff with the enrollment-based funding they get from the New York City school system.

But the building council would never be able to run Richman as efficiently or effectively as it does if it didn't have a large measure of autonomy from New York City's school headquarters in Brooklyn—autonomy, given the intensely bureaucratic and hierarchical nature of New York's public school system, that the complex's founders had to work long and hard to win. And even with a substantial amount of independence the council has had to get the bureaucracy's blessing before moving on several matters. The city's superintendent of alternative schools, for example, would only let the Richman council take out the building's metal detectors and surveillance cameras once the council had demonstrated that it had the backing of parents to do so.

Nor would Richman be the place it is today if Meier and

her colleagues hadn't won the support of the 140,000-member United Federation of Teachers (UFT), the city's influential teachers union.

The UFT, like many teachers unions, has the power to effectively veto school closings under job security provisos in its contract with the city's school board. Meier thus sought the support of Sandra Feldman, the UFT president, in the early planning stages of the Richman complex. The working conditions of UFT teachers in Richman were terrible, she told Feldman, and the multiplex was a solution to the problem.

Feldman, who is now the president of the American Federation of Teachers, the UFT's parent organization, agreed to the Richman conversion and the UFT arranged early retirement packages and transfers to other schools for departing Richman staff.

Just as importantly, a couple of years before the Julia Richman complex opened, the UFT and the New York City school board negotiated a revolutionary pact that offered the city's schools autonomy—rare in public education—over staffing, schedules, and other key aspects of school life. Under the so-called School Based Options agreement, schools with at least 70 percent of teachers backing the concept are able to abandon seniority-based staffing and other union-negotiated strictures. As a result, Richman schools can hire teachers who share the schools' educational philosophies, which greatly strengthens the schools' sense of community.

Of course, replacing the nation's many dysfunctional large urban high schools with smaller, more personal educational settings such as those in the new Richman complex doesn't guarantee students a high-quality education. Such settings are a critical part of the school reform puzzle. But strong teaching is also key to students' success. Acknowledging that fact, Richman's new schools have sought to take advantage of their size to introduce instructional innovations that wouldn't be possible in many large schools. Urban, Vanguard, and Manhattan International, for example, use a student-evaluation system that requires every student to make oral defenses of science, social studies, math, and several other projects that they must complete in addition to their regular courses to graduate.

But despite its successes, the Richman complex is under tremendous pressure to conform to the priorities of the larger New York City school system in ways that threaten Richman's stability.

A couple of years ago New York City's education bureaucracy put school guards under the jurisdiction of the city's police department. As a result, any statements that students make to security guards can be used against the students in disciplinary hearings—a fact, says Bill Ling, the director of Manhattan International, that "undercuts students' trust in Richman."

The week I visited Richman, the bureaucracy assigned a new guidance counselor to Ling's school, "bumping" Manhattan International's existing counselor out of a job during the height of the college-admissions season. The counselor claimed the job under a clause in the UFT's collective bargaining contract that permits teachers in schools with declining enrollments to take the jobs of less-experienced teachers in other schools. "I'm the principal and I have no say," Ling objected at the time. But he protested to the city's school authorities and the carpetbagger counselor was sent elsewhere. The year before, a city school administrator sent a patronage hire to be Richman's technology specialist, despite the individual's having scant technology experience. The building council turned down the funding for the job rather than take the person.

And school authorities repeatedly have sought to put more students in Richman's high schools in response to charges by the city's large, traditional high schools that Richman's schools are underpopulated. Richman's schools don't conform to the city's students-per-square-foot regulations, the large schools argue, though there are presently more students in Richman—1,800—than there were before its transformation into a multiplex, when Richman was substantially underpopulated. "There's always pull toward the center, toward bureaucratic control," says Mack. "What we do is not really understandable to a bureaucracy."

Recently a group of parents sought to dismantle the Richman complex completely. In a confrontation where race and class were never far from the surface of the debate, the mostly white and affluent parents of students at a nearby elementary school for gifted students pressed local politicians to have Richman turned into a single, "zoned" high school available only to Upper East Side students, a move that would have excluded from Richman the many students who now travel to the complex from Harlem, Manhattan's Lower East Side, and the Bronx.

Richman fought back, led by Ann Cook, who as Richman's Project Director expends as much energy on behalf of Richman outside the complex as Mack expends within the building.

The building council organized against the so-called Partnership for an Upper East Side High School and on the council's behalf Cook sought the help of Richman's "board of advisors," a panel of influential New York lawyers, corporate executives, foundation officers, civil rights leaders, labor unionists, and university professors that the council had assembled years earlier to help navigate New York's political waters. "Like most bureaucracies, the New York board of education responds to outside pressure, not to middle management," says Cook. Together, the Richman building council and its influential backers worked the city's educational and political leaders and the attack on Richman ended with the parent group being "given" a building twelve blocks north of Richman.

Ultimately, Richman's leaders don't take much of anything for granted when it comes to preserving the Richman complex. At the start of every school year Mack gathers the new teachers from throughout the complex to explain Richman and how it works. "You have to keep building culture," he says. "It's not automatic."

But to engineer Broderick the results speak for themselves. "After forty-two years in the business," he says of the transformation at Richman, "it's the first time I've ever had to ask teachers to leave their rooms at the end of the day so I can clean."

2 Engaging Debates

Urban Academy,
New York City

There was the relentless din of the Manhattan street a single story below. And the desks in Avram Barlowe's and Herb Mack's social studies class were pressed together so tightly in a circle around the room's periphery that it was tough for students to stand up once they had climbed into place. But the assembled students—twenty-eight sophomores, juniors, and seniors—were oblivious to the distractions. They were debating passionately the week's topic, scrawled on one of the seventy-nine-year-old classroom's old-fashioned blackboards: "B----, N-----, F---: How should people respond when words like these are used?"

"Words are only words, what matters is the way they're used," suggested a student with a thick gold chain and a baseball cap on backwards. "If a friend says, 'Fuck you,' it's OK, he's just joking around."

"Yeah, it's about context," said April, an African American classmate. "'What's up, bitch?' is OK. It depends on who says it and how."

"People have a right to speak if they want to," suggested Juan Carlos, a senior.

"Freedom of speech should not extend to hate speech," countered Mack, trying to be provocative.

"Nigger, nigger, nigger, nigger, nigger, nigger. I've said it six times and I'm white. What are you going to do about it, Herb?" responded a girl named Zarina, wryly.

"OK, OK," interjected a classmate. "But freedom of speech is tricky. You have to deal with the consequences of what you say. You really can't just say anything."

A half an hour later the debate was going strong. Nearly every student had contributed, bound only by the small sand timer on Mack's desk, which he turned over when a student started speaking. Over the next week the students would research and write papers on the topic they were debating. And then, in subsequent weeks, they would move on to other tough questions. Should society jail athletes for violent acts committed during an athletic contest? Should governments have the power to execute people? Is a public figure's personal life any of our business?

They tackled these boulder-sized subjects in a course

aptly named "Looking for an Argument?," one of the most popular at Urban Academy Laboratory High School, a 120-student institution that has been strikingly successful in using classroom debates to engage some of New York City's most challenging students in demanding academics, students who have transferred to Urban after struggling academically and socially at the city's other high schools.

Classroom debate and discussion are nothing new, of course. But in American public education courses that rely heavily on those teaching strategies—courses that make students' voices the linchpin of instruction—have traditionally been reserved for advanced students. In a majority of high school classes, particularly those serving the disadvantaged, students play largely passive roles; teachers' lessons are linear and given as gospel. Teachers move from A to B to C, and C is nearly always set in advance: The South's dependency on slave labor led to the secession of the southern states, which led to the start of the Civil War.

Urban, founded in the mid-1980s and now located in a second-story wing of the Julia Richman Educational Complex on Manhattan's Upper East Side, has rejected that conventional public education strategy for teaching disadvantaged students. Its students have to gather and evaluate their own evidence, develop and defend their own ideas, and come to their own conclusions. One hears over and over at Urban, "Can you give me an example of that?" "What's your evidence?" "Where do you stand on that?" "Do you agree with what's been said?" "Am I hearing a difference of opinion?"

"We're continually trying to get kids to see things from different points of view, and thereby develop their own points of view, based on evidence," says Ann Cook, Urban's cofounder. A colleague of Cook's, the educator Deborah Meier, developed the strategy known as Inquiry Learning in the mid-1980s.

It's on display in nearly every Urban Academy classroom. When I visited the school, students in Harry Feder's criminal law class were wrestling with the legality of a recent New York City Police Department drug bust. Detectives had discovered a crop of marijuana plants thriving under high-intensity lamps in a Brooklyn house after training heat detectors on the house from the street.

"Detecting heat through the wall of a house isn't a 'search,'" argued a student. "So it can't be illegal."

"It's an invasion of privacy," retorted a classmate. "The heat could be coming from anything—the oven, radiators, anything."

"The occupant does have a prior criminal record, and his wife has been arrested for growing pot in the past," a third student noted, suggesting that the police had probable cause to surveil the house, as horns blared on Sixty-seventh Street.

"How's the use of a heat detector the same or different from a wire tap?" asked Feder, stoking the debate.

Even math teachers, traditionally the most lecture-oriented teachers in high schools, use Inquiry strategies at Urban.

In a routine that's present in every Urban math class, students in Becky Walzer's geometry course worked animatedly in groups of three or four to calculate the areas of shapes as Walzer sketched them on the board. Quick discussions and occasional debates produced an answer per group on sheets of paper that were passed to Walzer, who graded them and posted each group's results on the blackboard. If a group got an answer wrong, or if students had questions, she worked through the problem from the front of the class. Then it was on to the next problem.

The competition raged on through the end of the class, when Walzer tallied the results and declared a winner among the groups. The victors pumped their fists. The losers grumbled. But they would be back in action the next day, when the groups would be reconfigured for another round of competition.

By putting students at the center of its classrooms in this way, Urban has made learning engaging for the many students at the school who had been thoroughly disenchanted by the dry, teacher-centric pedagogy that pervades many American high schools. In the words of math teacher Wally Warshawsky: "If you lecture, the first five kids get it and everyone else sleeps. With Inquiry, they have to engage."

Urban's Inquiry strategy also draws students into the

45

academic life of the school by signaling to them that what they have to say matters, that their classroom contributions are valued. "In most schools disadvantaged kids are in classes where their voices aren't part of the equation," says cofounder Cook. "Urban students, in contrast, have a sense of ownership of the process. It's you figuring out what YOU think about issues." Even the placement of desks in Urban's classrooms—in large, inward-facing circles, as in Barlowe's and Mack's argument course, or pushed together in threes and fours, as in Walzer's geometry course—are designed to engage students. So are snappy course titles like "Looking for an Argument?," "Just Bill" (Shakespeare), "Frontiers and Borderlands" (history of the American West), and "Heat" (chemistry and physics).

Gail Lemelbaum's fiction class is a measure of Urban's success with the strategy. Three students sat sullenly at the beginning of the class, weighed down by gold chains, baggy pants, and give-me-space demeanors. But then, in response to a question to the class by Lemelbaum about Jerzy Kosinski's portrayal of German soldiers in his novel *The Painted Bird,* one of the students inclined to silence suddenly presented a smart point of view and a passage in the book to back it up.

Cook argues that Inquiry Learning is a more intellectually honest teaching strategy than traditional, teacher-centered instruction. "In traditional classrooms teachers are in effect trying to sell students on a particular way of looking at material," she argues. "In truth, there are many ways of looking at a problem. Inquiry acknowledges that."

The dozen or so students in Terri Grosso's "Chemical Puzzles" class proved Cook's point. As they tested whether various solutions were acids or bases, Grosso asked, "What if I have a solution and I add phenol saline and it turns pink? What do I know?"

"That it's a base," a student replied.

"If you put enough phenol saline in the solution," another suggested.

"Yeah, but the more phenol you add, the darker the solution gets," protested senior Jarvis Idowu, a first generation American who had transferred to Urban from Brooklyn Friends School. "You end up with just the color of the indicator."

"Is that a problem with our experiment?" Grosso asked.

"Yes, we should be measuring the amount of the solution and the phenol that we add," concluded April Chapple, a junior.

"Yeah, we won't get consistent results if everyone doesn't put the same amount in," concurred Chapple's classmate, Nels Valdez.

"Next time." Grosso smiled, as the class ended.

"At my old school," Jarvis said afterward, "they stick a lot of stuff in your head and make you regurgitate it at the end of the year. It's like storing stuff on a computer. Here, they teach you how to think for yourself. They teach you how to ask the right questions."

Outside Grosso's room, the hallway walls are covered with student art, including a strikingly evocative series of photographs of New York City graffiti. Not surprisingly, art, a powerful vehicle for personal expression, is big at Urban.

The constant give and take in Urban's classrooms creates more tolerant as well as more independent-minded students. Urban students learn to expect their perspectives to be challenged and aren't threatened by that reality. They learn to distinguish between opposing points of view and personal attacks. They learn to judge one another on the strengths of their arguments.

At one point during Harry Feder's criminal law class a student blurted out, "Fuck you," to a classmate who rebutted his argument effectively. But other students intervened. "That's not cool," said a classmate of the student's profanity. Context does indeed matter.

To stress to students that any point of view can be debated dispassionately, Barlowe and Mack begin each Argument debate by briefly arguing opposite sides of the question of the day, after students select which side each teacher takes. Urban's teachers say that the culture of tolerance that Inquiry promotes has contributed significantly to the low rates of disciplinary infractions at the inner city school.

48

Urban's Inquiry-based courses tend to cover fewer topics in greater depth than those in traditional high schools. But the school nonetheless expects students to develop substantial knowledge of core subjects in the process of answering the big questions that Urban courses pose to students.

That's no less the case in Urban's off-beat "mini" courses than it is in its Shakespeare and chemistry classes. Feder and Walzer recently teamed up to teach a between-semesters course called "Racing at the Track," in which students confronted such questions as "Are jockeys athletes?," "Is excessive gambling a disease, as dangerous as alcohol or drug addiction?," and "Is there any skill involved in betting?" To write essays on those subjects students read the histories of great racehorses and jockeys; learned the mathematics of pari-mutuel betting; went as a class to Aqueduct Racetrack, off-track betting offices, and horse farms; and interviewed breeders, trainers, track handicappers, jockeys, a member of Gambler's Anonymous, and a Yale statistician.

"Content," says cofounder Cook, "is important." What sets Urban apart is that the school expects students to apply knowledge and information, not merely acquire it.

But Inquiry Learning's expectation that students play leading roles in the classroom isn't easy for every student. "For those who are used to having their teachers tell them what to think, Inquiry is very stressful," says Grosso. When I visited Urban, a student in Warshawsky's probability class pleaded with Warshawsky to show the class how to compute an answer. "No," the teacher replied, matter-of-factly, "figure it out with your group." Another student later asked, "How can that be the answer if...?" "Ah, that's the question," Warshawsky responded, to the student's evident frustration.

Urban takes steps to ensure that students have a sense of the school's strategies and expectations before they arrive. It requires prospective students to spend a day attending classes, do logic problems, write essays, and have interviews with students and teachers—even though the school admits every applicant, space permitting.

But even the students who aren't deterred by such demands sometime struggle once they enter Urban's student-centered classrooms.

The beginning of Walzer's Writing Workshop class, with an enrollment of mostly newer students, was painful to watch as Walzer gamely attempted to get students talking about a passage they had read from Piri Thomas's autobiography of life in Harlem, *Down These Mean Streets*.

"Reactions?" she asked.

"It's boring."

"Why?"

"It just is."

"Sylvia, what do you think?

"It's boring."

"Why?"

The student shrugged her shoulders.

"When you find it's boring you need to push yourself to ask why, so you can avoid the same problems in your own writing," Walzer responded.

By the end of the hour-long class students had begun to engage—but only because Walzer is a skilled Inquiry teacher and she stuck with the task until her students eventually responded.

Yet finding teachers like Walzer is a challenge for Urban, Cook says. Public school teachers are more often trained to talk at students rather than to listen to what they are saying. Many aren't comfortable sharing the stage with their students; it's hard work, unpredictable, and there's a greater risk of students exposing gaps in teachers' knowledge.

It certainly would have been easier for Grosso to simply recite Newton's Third Law of Physics when a student in her Mechanics class asked a couple of days before I visited Urban, "If I push on something, is it pushing back?" Instead of giving students the Third Law and moving on to the day's topic, Grosso put a book on a table in the classroom and asked if the table was pushing up on the book. Students spent the entire period reaching a consensus that it did. Only then did Grosso give them Newton's law: that for every action, there is an equal and opposite reaction.

"Inquiry classes frequently don't go in the direction that you're planning," Grosso said with a chuckle, recalling the class.

It's probably not by coincidence that Harry Feder, a former lawyer, is one of Urban's best teachers. Having spent years as a litigator, he's adept at drawing ideas and insights out of students. He instinctively asks students the right questions.

Because there aren't a lot of college students trained to manage Inquiry classrooms, Urban trains many of its teachers itself.

It uses two strategies.

Under the first, it invites talented teacher candidates at New York–area colleges to student-teach at Urban for a year with an eye to making the best of them permanent staff members. When I visited Urban, Shuba Satyaprasad, a student in the master's program at Teachers College, Columbia University, was leading a spirited discussion in her History of Ancient India class on the question, "What's an advanced society?" Barlowe was in the classroom, busily taking notes on how Satyaprasad asked questions, how she focused the conversation, and how she ensured that every student participated. He was there, and at each of Satyaprasad's classes, as Satyaprasad's mentor. In turn, Satyaprasad, who had spent two years as a lawyer before enrolling at Teachers College, was a regular observer of Barlowe's American history classes. Then, at the end of every week, they met to share notes.

Barlowe's work with Satyaprasad represented a significant investment by Urban in the former lawyer. But by the year's end she was a strong Inquiry teacher.

Urban launched its second teacher-training strategy in the mid-1990s, when the school helped to establish a two-year, state-sanctioned School-Based Teacher Education Program that allows teacher candidates to earn a state teaching license by working at Urban or other select public schools. Rather than study "methods" courses and other traditional education school fare, the STEP students coteach Inquiry-based courses with senior Urban teachers, audit the teaching of several other of Urban's best instructors, tutor Urban students, and study educational issues at the school. A quarter of Urban's teachers are STEP graduates.

They and the rest of the Urban staff then spend Friday afternoons throughout each school year working together on Inquiry instructional strategies—another major Urban investment in teacher training. In one session that I watched, Warshawsky and three colleagues talked through Warshawsky's misgivings that his Probability and Statistics students were saying in class discussions that because they read studies that the findings must be true. "I'd like to get more conflict among experts into our reading," Warshawsky said, "to show the kids that even in scholarly journals there's a lot of disagreement, a lot of different interpretations of evidence. They need to know that in many cases both sides are partially right and partially wrong."

As important to Urban's achievements as its cultivation of a new type of teacher has been the school's creation of a new way of measuring student performance.

"You want to make sure a school's teaching and the way it's measuring students' work are linked—that's basic pedagogy," Cook says. "If you are teaching kids to weigh evidence, express awareness of multiple perspectives, organize information, make connections, speculate on alternatives, and assess the value of ideas they've encountered, then you have to have assessments that allow students to demonstrate that they can do those things."

Most standardized tests, however, don't measure such skills, or do so superficially. They place students in the largely passive role of identifying right answers supplied by others. They rarely evaluate students' abilities to apply what they've learned.

That's perhaps not the worst thing if one's measuring basic skills in the elementary grades. But it's a serious problem in a high school like Urban, Cook and her colleagues contend. "If you have a narrow test," says Cook, "you'll have narrow teaching."

So Urban evaluates its students differently than traditional public high schools. In addition to graded report cards students receive narrative reports twice a semester in each of their courses, and at the end of each semester each student meets with two teachers to review the student's semester work.

And to graduate Urban students need not only a sufficient grade point average. They must also successfully complete a series of seven "proficiencies" that require students to do independent research projects in literature, mathematics, science, social studies, creative arts, criticism, and library usage—and then present the projects orally to panels of Urban teachers and/or outside experts.

The projects, also known as "performance assessments" in education parlance, build on students' course work. Each one has several course prerequisites. Students, for example, must complete algebra and geometry before they undertake the math proficiency.

The projects range in duration from several months to over a year and can take the form of papers, presentations, or experiments. In creative arts, for example, students present, publish, or exhibit their work together with a written analysis of it.

Most students complete the projects during their junior and senior years. They become part of a student's graduation "portfolio."

Urban has a set of "rubrics" that the school's teachers and outside experts use in evaluating students' proficiencies. They score everything from students' use of proper grammar in the literature paper to their application of the "scientific method" in the science proficiency. Students have to earn cumulative scores of "outstanding," "good," or "competent" to pass proficiencies. Even though students work closely with their advisors on their proficiency projects,

Urban's evaluators aren't reluctant to require revisions in the work that's presented to them—a fact that contributes to about 10 percent of Urban's students having to spend an extra semester at the school before they're able to graduate.

Rachel Casado-Alba, a senior who traveled an hour each way to Urban from the Bronx, did her literature proficiency on Margaret Atwood's *The Handmaid's Tale*. She started the book early in the school year, she told me, discussing its themes several times with Urban teacher Rachel Wyatt, her advisor. Then, in January, she traveled to Lower Manhattan for a ninety-minute session with Judith Walzer, a literature professor at the New School for Social Research, one of many New York City professors and other professionals who serve as external assessors. Urban has enlisted their participation to ensure that students' proficiency projects are held to high standards and to signal to students that Urban takes the proficiency program seriously. Walzer asked Rachel to discuss the plot, characters, themes, and other aspects of Atwood's novel. Rachel rode the subway home that night anxious about her performance, only to learn in a telephone call from Barnes several days later that she had passed the proficiency.

Junior Erik Osaben, meanwhile, spent several hours a week for three months working on a science proficiency on how eye color is inherited in flies. He had to breed flies and chart the frequency with which certain eye colors were passed down to subsequent generations. Then he had to compare his findings to those in established research and explain—both in a paper and in an oral presentation—discrepancies between those results and his own.

Urban's students, many of them street-hardened and emotionally guarded, tackle the proficiencies with surprising enthusiasm.

When I visited, a student I'll call Carlos Rojas, an East Harlem senior who was in and out of shelters as a kid, was posting flyers around the school inviting students to watch his oral presentation of his criticism proficiency later in the day. A teacher who happened by asked Rojas if he'd had a good response. "Yeah," he responded, excitedly.

After the school day ended eight students and four teachers gathered at the back of a classroom. Rojas, wearing baggy blue jeans, an oversized, untucked checkered shirt, and a wisp of a goatee, faced the audience, standing next to a projector loaded with slides of the lithographs of Carol Walker, a contemporary African American artist whose subjects include blacks in stereotypical slave roles.

"I didn't like Walker's work because she caters to white stereotypes," Rojas told the assemblage, as he projected images of Walker's work on a screen. "She made light of slavery."

But he had changed his mind about the work in the course of his project, he said, because he began to under-

stand that Walker didn't necessarily agree with the stereotypes simply because they appeared in her work. He had
reached that conclusion by reading the published criticism
of Walker's work, observing her work in Manhattan galleries, and interviewing the galleries' owners.

Rojas's presentation lasted twenty minutes. Then his
audience started asking questions. "Maybe Walker's drawing attention to slavery by making us mad about these pictures," one student suggested. "I'm not sure I see the
pictures the same way you do," challenged another.

Rojas responded earnestly for nearly an hour. He didn't
grasp every nuance of every question. And his interpretations of Walker's work tended to be pretty literal. But given
Rojas's academic history his presentation wasn't bad: When
he came to Urban he could barely read or write.

It's a big deal at Urban when a student "gets" a proficiency. The student's faculty advisor often rings a bell as the
student walks the length of the school's corridor. Students
and teachers stand in classroom doorways and "hoot, holler,
and shout," says Casado-Able. "It's embarrassing," she says,
"but fun." By the end of the school year such events take
place nearly every day.

But Urban's proficiencies don't jibe very well with New
York State's graduation tests, which are mostly fact-based,
multiple-choice assessments of the sort that Cook and her
colleagues say harm Urban's Inquiry instruction.

Back in 1995, Urban and other New York State high

schools using performance measures won a five-year exemption from the state's Regents tests in math, social studies, foreign language, and science. But in an April 25, 2001, ruling New York State commissioner of education Richard Mills refused to extend the waiver. There wasn't enough evidence to judge whether the schools' performance tests were as good as the state's Regents exams at measuring students' grasp of the four subjects, Mills declared. He rejected the recommendation of his own panel of national testing experts that the exemption be extended while the state study the question.

As a result, students entering Urban and the other schools in 2001–02 as ninth graders were required to pass Regents exams in the four subjects and English to earn a diploma.

But the schools have taken on the commissioner's ruling with the same zeal that pervades many of Urban's classrooms. Organized as the New York Performance Standards Consortium, they have put the matter before the state's top court, where it's pending. They have drafted legislation, introduced by Assemblyman Ruben Diaz Jr. of the Bronx in the spring of 2002, that would permit school systems or groups of schools such as the consortium to opt out of Regents testing if their student attendance, drop-out, and college-placement records are stronger than state averages. And in late 2002, a joint legislative panel held hearings on the Regents tests at the consortium's urging.

Predictably, Urban's students have been in the middle of the debate. Tacked to the wall in the school's central gathering area are placards from a rally that students and teachers held in Albany, the state capital, to protest Mills's ruling. "Mills' 3 R's," says one, "Read, Remember, Regurgitate." "Bubble Tests=Bubble Brains," says another.

So far, Urban hasn't changed its curriculum substantially in the wake of the Mills ruling. It has only added a couple of days of preparation for the Regents tests. But the pressure to teach students a wide array of fact-based information tested by the Regents exams—names and dates and formulas— and to do so at the expense of classroom debates and proficiency projects, is great, say Urban's teachers.

It would be ironic if the Regents tests forced Urban to shift its teaching strategies. Commissioner Mills has demanded that students at Urban take the Regents test as part of a larger campaign to ensure high standards in New York's public schools. That's surely a worthy goal. But student attendance at Urban is 91 percent, sharply higher than the 82 percent in high schools citywide. Only about 3 percent of the school's students drop out a year. And 95 percent of Urban's graduates earn admission to four-year colleges. They attend city and state universities and alternative liberal arts schools like Hampshire, Beloit, and Goucher, and they also attend academic powerhouses like Wesleyan, Swarthmore, Oberlin, Barnard, and the University of Chicago.

That's not a bad record for any school, much less one that educates second-chance students.

It's a record that derives largely from Urban's departures from the comprehensive high school model—its staffing and instructional autonomy, its self-selected students, and, in particular, its smallness. Those features have combined to create a strikingly strong sense of community at Urban. That has led to a safe school and a school with a coherent and strongly shared academic vision. It's hard to imagine the entire staff of a traditional comprehensive high school working together to perfect a schoolwide teaching strategy the way Urban teachers do. It's also hard to imagine that many students in comprehensive high schools would buy into Urban's teaching strategy, with its expectation that students routinely hold up their work to public scrutiny. Only students who trust the adults and the other students around them would subject themselves to such risks. And it's in small, close-knit school communities like Urban— rather than large, comprehensive high schools—where such trust is most readily nurtured.

3 **Getting Real**

High Tech High, San Diego, California

When I met Kyle McDonald it would have been easy to think he was doing what's typical of teenagers today: playing a computer game. As the San Diego tenth grader worked a keyboard and a mouse, a ghoulish creature materialized on a monitor.

But Kyle, a lanky fifteen-year-old who sported cargo pants, sneakers, and braces, wasn't playing a game. He was making one. He was constructing a monstrous being out of cones, spheres, cubes, and other geometric shapes as part of an ambitious project to create an animated game to teach students keyboarding. Eventually, the creature would become one of many that students would blast from their screens during touch-typing exercises.

Yet Kyle wasn't a computer prodigy, and I didn't find him slaving away in a software hothouse. Instead, he was in a computer lab at High Tech High, a bold new high school that has put technology at the center of an inventive educational strategy: teaching students academic subjects through a series of independent and group projects. At many high schools technology is treated as a vocation, as a subject to be studied; at High Tech High, students use technology to learn geometry, biology, history, and other traditional subjects in a markedly different way.

High Tech High opened with two hundred ninth and tenth graders in the fall of 2000 under a charter from the San Diego public school system, drawing its students from throughout the San Diego metro area, and has since added eleventh and twelfth grades and is now fully enrolled at four hundred students. As a "charter school" it is publicly funded but largely independent of San Diego school authorities.

High Tech High's founder and the designer of its technology-based teaching strategy is Larry Rosenstock, a transplanted Bostonian with a career as unconventional as his new school. A carpenter turned lawyer turned vocational-education teacher, he became principal of the Rindge Manual Training School, a leading technical high school in Cambridge, Massachusetts, in 1990. After Rindge merged with 350-year-old scholastic powerhouse Cambridge Latin he ran the combined school in the mid-1990s, before leaving to lead a federally funded study of urban high schools.

Rosenstock says that the study and his many years in vocational education taught him that urban high schools that successfully educate students outside of the academic elite share two qualities: They establish respectful, adultlike environments for students, and they work hard to make academics relevant to students' lives. "Too much of the traditional high school curriculum today is made up of fragmented and decontextualized knowledge that doesn't have any meaning for many students," he says. "Project-based learning works because it gives students a reason to embrace the academic curriculum; they recognize that they have to know math or history or physics to complete their projects."

Technology, Rosenstock says, is a catalyst for the hands-on learning that he favors. "It's a tool," he said, eating a peanut butter and jelly sandwich and drinking a Dr. Pepper at his desk at High Tech High.

Such thinking has led Rosenstock to design a high school that is physically and organizationally very different from the norm in America, a small, coherent learning community, where nearly every aspect of school life promotes a distinctive educational strategy.

High Tech High is housed in a renovated warehouse on a sprawling former Navy training base a couple of miles from downtown San Diego. Half the building is a vast open space under thirty-five-foot-high, sky-lit ceilings, from which hang brightly painted ducts and drop lighting. The space is divided with waist-high walls into four "work station suites," each with clusters of desks and Internet-linked computers for twenty-eight students. Each suite also has a glassed-in classroom with conventional high school desks for the same number of students. Because of the low partitions, one can stand just about anywhere and watch the goings-on throughout the Great Room, as the large open space is called.

The other half of Rosenstock's warehouse high school contains traditional offices for Rosenstock and other administrators; half a dozen conventional classrooms (each with a "Smart Board," a four-foot by six-foot screen on the wall that projects the contents of a laptop computer); and laboratories for mechanical engineering, biotechnology, video production, and animation.

The way students spend their days at High Tech High is as different as where they spend them. School starts late, at 8:45 in the morning, in response to new research showing that adolescents need a lot more sleep than they typically get, and runs until 3:45 in the afternoon. In place of traditional attendance-taking, students and teachers "scan-in" a fingerprint when they arrive in the morning. When I was at High Tech High the first half of the day was broken into two blocks. One day they would spend an hour-and-a-half on humanities and another hour-and-a-half on mathematics, often in the school's classrooms. The next day they would study math and had "independent setting," an hour-and-a-half of independent computer time, where they would work on a wide range of projects at their workstations. The third day they would have independent setting and humanities. And then they would repeat the progression.

Each afternoon brought another three hours of project work under the tutelage of nine "project teachers," generalists who helped students on a range of individual and group initiatives in a role akin to that of athletic coaches. Because the school's server permits any student or teacher to log on at any computer in the building, students often migrated to different parts of the Great Room during project periods, with the school's blessing. There was, as a result, a very informal atmosphere during project periods—and a great deal of informal teaching and learning going on between students. In many ways, High Tech High seemed more like a high-tech workplace than a school.

Kyle McDonald was working in the school's animation lab during my visit. In the Great Room I met Yasmin Rahman, a ninth grader with long, jet-black hair and a shy smile. She and two classmates were deciphering an electrical diagram so they could build a "current board" that they would use to remote-control a yellow robot about the size of a playground dump truck. Eventually, said project advisor Ben

Daly, a twenty-seven-year-old physics graduate from Haver-
ford College, Jasmin and the others would maneuver the robot via the Internet, using a computer chip that they would
program themselves.

At the other end of the building project teacher Lee
Walters had gathered nineteen students in a conference
room to discuss one of the school's largest projects: a documentary on the decommissioned Navy base around High
Tech High. The sprawling complex was about to be razed
and put to commercial and residential uses and High Tech
High's students and staff had hit on the idea of preserving
the base's past in a documentary.

Technology would be at the center of the students' work.
They would use the Internet to search the San Diego and
Navy archives for photographs and other material for a book
on the base's history and its decommissioning at the end of
the Cold War, which they would design themselves using
desktop publishing software. And they would make a digital
documentary film about the base that they would edit on
computers in the school's video-production lab. To record
the base's demolition, they would use a computer-as-
sisted drafting program called AutoCAD to design a robot
equipped with a video camera, because students wouldn't
be permitted to wander around the base once demolition
had begun. Students would also communicate their work a
third way, through a website.

Walters, a chemistry Ph.D. and university professor turned high school teacher, ran a no-nonsense meeting. He sounded like a corporate CEO.

"Where are we finding people to interview?" he wanted to know.

"Here are sample ads that we've written for three local newspapers asking Navy veterans to talk about their time at the base," responded ninth grader Van Whiting.

Walters nodded. "Film people, I've got four documentaries here for you to watch and I've ordered screenplays for two of them. I want you to study the relationship between the screenplays and the films. For tomorrow, I want you to report on how filmmakers use storyboards."

Then a screen descended at one end of the conference room and two students gave a PowerPoint presentation outlining how they planned to document the base's demolition photographically.

Technology helps promote the adultlike atmosphere at High Tech High that Rosenstock values by increasing students' opportunities to be self-sufficient learners. In particular, many High Tech High students use the Internet to do advanced work independently. Zak Zelin, an easy-going ninth grader ("I'm last on every list") with spiky, blue-green hair, was among them. He had already completed a conventional honors algebra class in the first four months of the school year and Jeff Blount, his teacher, had sent him to the

Internet in pursuit of advanced work. His textbook was the Yahoo search engine. With it, he found sites like www.algebra.com where there were plenty of tough problems.

To further promote the adult-ness of the High Tech High educational experience—and to help students grasp the relevance of what they are studying—students must complete an off-campus internship of at least one hundred hours during their junior or senior years. Most students are placed by Caleb Clark, the school's full-time internship coordinator, with San Diego's 715 high-technology companies. But being at technology sites isn't necessarily the point. "The key is connecting kids to adults," says Rosenstock. "As John Dewey would say, occupations offer a context, not an outcome."

Treating students as adults rather than adolescents, in part by having them build relationships with adults who are making use of academic material in their work lives, pays tangible dividends, Rosenstock says. The federally funded study he headed found that urban students with well-constructed internships went to college at significantly higher rates than those who lacked strong mentor relationships with adults.

Technology also pays other, more modest, dividends at High Tech High. Though big advances in computer hardware and software and the rise of the Internet have turned many heads in recent years, one of the first educational uses of computers—for tutoring in basic skills—continues to be a valuable one, says Walters. "Computer tutorials are step-by-step, and individualized; they take students where they are and build from there." Students studying math, typing, and Spanish are among those who routinely use such tutorials at High Tech High.

Also, says Walters, a slight, quietly intense man with wire-rimmed glasses and closely shorn gray hair, word-processing technology makes students more facile editors and thus encourages them to draft and redraft written work, a valuable part of learning to write effectively, but one that students who have to rely on bad handwriting and even typewriters often shun. "The screen is a great leveler among students," says Rob Riordon, a former teacher at Rindge and Latin and now a consultant to High Tech High.

And though technology is first and foremost a learning tool at High Tech High, the school requires students to think reflectively about how they deploy technology in their studies. Each trimester they have to select three technologies that they've used in their projects—digital cameras, say, or the Internet—and report on several things about each technology, including how they would use the technology more effectively in the same project if they were to repeat the project. During my visit, Branden Lundy, one of biology teacher Leslie Woollenweber's students, was embarking on a project that contemplated technology in a particularly innovative way: he was going to compare a computer virus to a human virus, contrasting, for example, how the two viruses are transmitted and how they affect their hosts.

Nor does High Tech High's emphasis on technology-as-tool mean that students don't learn about technology per se at the school. Though there aren't any courses on web design, say, or the BASIC programming language (the school's single technology course—in Cisco network training—is taught after school), the school supplies the software for such programs to students, who tend to teach it to themselves or to each other as they need the skills in the course of completing their projects. Rosenstock estimates, for example, that half of High Tech High students can design web pages using Dreamweaver software.

It's the culture at High Tech High—the school's project-based teaching strategy and its emphasis on student self-sufficiency—that leads many students to acquire tech skills themselves, says architect and teacher David Stephen, a former High Tech High administrator who helped design the school. High Tech High, he says, does not admit only technophiles. Yes, the school has a hackers club and one of its members, within a span of a week, worked his way into both Stephen's e-mail account and the school's financial files. And the school does require applicants to demonstrate a pretty strong desire to be in a technology environment (students have to apply to the school, attend an on-site orientation, write an essay about why they want to go to High Tech

High, and have a parent or guardian and two teachers or counselors write to the school on their behalf). But the school admits students with a wide range of academic abilities ("Some are reading and writing at the third and fourth grade levels, some could go to college next week," says Stephen) and about a third of High Tech High's students don't have computers at home. About a third also come from families on public assistance. Only about a fifth of the school's students are technology wonks, the sorts of students who might have business cards for web design and software security businesses that they run after school.

Apart from its overarching attempt to use technology as a catalyst for project-based learning, High Tech High is trying out other new uses of technology in education. It is conducting experiments within an experiment.

One of them involves pilot testing a digital humanities textbook for a division of publishing giant Houghton Mifflin. Jeff Robins's world history students spent two weeks just before I visited the school studying Napoleon and the French Revolution using a "textbook" that existed only on the Internet. The Houghton Mifflin subsidiary put the entire multimedia instructional unit—complete with animated battle maps and audio renditions by actors of statements by key historical figures like Marie Antoinette—on an Internet system built strictly for Robins's class. "The effect," says Robins, "was to bring the period to life for students in ways that traditional paper textbooks simply can't."

Rosenstock and his staff have also built an electronic student tracking system, an endeavor that has put them on the cutting edge of a nationwide movement to report student performance more fully and more clearly.

In traditional comprehensive high schools, commentary on individual student performance is either fragmented (a student's math teacher never talks to the student's history teacher, say, or students' standardized testing reports aren't cycled back to the students' next year's teachers) or superficial (schools rarely publicize the level of difficulty of their courses, making it hard to gauge the significance of students' grades).

In response, High Tech High has created a "digital portfolio" for each student. Housed in the school's computer system, it includes traditional things such as students' transcripts and standardized test scores. But in an effort to paint a richer picture of students' learning experiences at the school the portfolios are also being designed to include "performance rubrics," measures of the school's "learning goals."

High Tech High has half a dozen "learning goals"—general themes and related "essential questions" that it hopes will inform the way students think about every subject they study. They include Collaboration ("How do I work with others?"); Technology ("How do I use technology as a tool?"); Communication ("How do I take in and express information?"); Art and Design ("How do I give shape and form to my ideas?"); Ethics and Responsibility ("How do my beliefs inform my actions?"); and Habits of Mind ("How do I think critically?"). The school's "performance rubrics" measure students' progress in each category.

High Tech High's staff has set standards for students in each category and then detailed what students must do to achieve the standards. In the "Communications" category, for example, students have to demonstrate their proficiency in "organization," "delivery," "audience," and "language." To make the grade in "organization," as an example, students have to make presentations that are "succinct," last for "an appropriate length of time," "convey a clear purpose," contain "smooth transitions" between elements, "build on main ideas," and end coherently. Jared Wells, High Tech High's assessment director, has developed templates that let teachers give students both numerical scores, on a scale of one to five, and written comments in every rubric subcategory.

Students also contribute to their digital portfolios, items such as their project reports, each trimester's reflections on the technology that they've used in their work, and other samples of the body of work that they build up at High Tech High. At the end of each school year students make presentations about what they've learned that year, using the contents of their portfolios as the basis for their presentations.

By gathering student-performance information in a single place and delivering it electronically, High Tech High's digital portfolios "help make the school's work more transparent," says Wells. Parents, for example, can review their kids' progress from anywhere via the Internet, and teachers with concerns about students can readily tap into other teachers' commentary on the students' performance. As a result, Wells says, digital portfolios promote constructive conversations about students. In contrast, he says, "paper reports frequently pile up and are forgotten."

Yet High Tech High's work to build a new-style high school with technology hasn't been without challenges. And High Tech High's responses to them are no less instructive than the innovations the school has achieved with technology in its short history.

Though students like Zak Zelin have used technology to push themselves academically (he and another student were doing the AutoCAD robot design for the Navy base documentary project), other High Tech High students haven't. A number of students weren't working particularly hard during their independent project time when I visited the school. "I'm just hanging out, I don't really have anything to do," a couple of students told me as I walked around the Great Room.

Nor have all students taken their digital portfolios seriously. During my visit a group of teachers gathered early in the morning to debate ways of encouraging students to put

more effort into their portfolio entries. After rejecting a sug-
gestion to make the quality of the portfolios a factor in students' humanities grades, they decided to make strong
portfolio work a "competency" that students would have
to meet to advance to the next grade. (The digital portfolios also have proven to be a burden for teachers. Because
they've had to write their performance-rubric responses on
paper and then enter them into the school's computer system, some haven't kept up with the task, "even among our
most conscientious teachers," says Wells. As a result, Wells
is planning to simplify teachers' work by putting rubric software on their laptop computers.

One reason for some students' failure to embrace technology on High Tech High's terms is that, in spite of the
school's attempts to explain its technology philosophy
to applicants, a significant number of students enter the
school believing that High Tech High is a technical school,
where they would learn about technology on the way to
more advanced training or a job in the San Diego high-tech
sector. "This isn't what I expected and it's not what I want,"
ninth grader Aaron Dimsdale told me, as he played fantasy
basketball on the Internet during his afternoon project
period. It's also difficult for students who have been taught
in traditional, teacher-led classrooms to adjust to High Tech
High's expectations that they use technology to be more
independent learners.

But Rosenstock, who, like his staff, wears a prefaded denim shirt with the High Tech High logo over the breast pocket, after the fashion at many high-tech firms, believes that the school was also responsible for some students' low levels of engagement. In early 2001, midway through the school's first year, he had already concluded that students' independent computer time wasn't "structured enough." Having a lot of powerful technology at their disposal wasn't enough, in the absence of more guidance from teachers, to spur students to be productive. In its second year, as a result, the school cut its three-hour afternoon project block in half and used the extra time to give students more formal instruction. A year later, in the fall of 2002, Rosenstock and his staff began having students do projects that were drawn directly from their course work, which led the school to eliminate independent project time in the Great Room for freshmen, sophomores, and juniors altogether. They now work in the Great Room when their subject-area teachers reserve the space for their students to do projects related to the topics they're studying in math, history, and other courses.

High Tech High, says David Stephen, hadn't done enough to ensure that student projects were sufficiently demanding. "Some teachers," he says, "weren't making projects rigorous enough, they weren't robust, in-depth." Even with state-of-the-art technology, designing high-quality independent projects requires a lot of hard work by teachers, High Tech High learned. In response, the school drew up prototypes of strong projects and trained its teachers to replicate their quality. It began having teachers of different subjects work together to create interdisciplinary projects. It added conventional courses in science. And some of the school's teachers began doing more traditional, front-of-the-classroom teaching to ensure that students learned key material. Biology teacher Woollenweber, for instance, started giving lectures on diseases and on environmental topics, trying to strike a balance between teacher-led learning and independent study. "The self-directed project work is critical," she told me when I visited the school. "It makes the subject matter interesting. And they aren't going to learn anything if they aren't motivated. But they also aren't going to get everything they need to know about immunology on their own."

Another hurdle for High Tech High—and for schools trying to replicate High Tech High's model—has been the $1.5 million price tag for the school's myriad technology. Rosenstock raised most of the money from outside sources, primarily high-tech entrepreneurs Irwin Jacobs, the co-founder of San Diego–based Qualcomm; his son, Gary Jacobs (the school's official title is the Gary and Jerri-Ann Jacobs High Tech High); and the State of California.

But Rosenstock also has taken steps at High Tech High

that have helped make the school's operating technology budget affordable: Because he believes that high schools should have only a limited number of instructional priorities, High Tech High has no athletic teams, marching bands, or art or music departments. It doesn't even have a gym or a cafeteria. As a result, the school spends less per student ($7,400 versus $7,600) than traditional San Diego public high schools, with lower student-teacher ratios.

Yet as High Tech High works to increase the rigor of its projects and to get all of its students using technology productively, it has had to spend additional money on teacher training. Says Riordon, the consultant, "You cannot be so invested in technology that you underinvest in human resources, because it's the human resources that are going to help kids use the technology wisely." Or as Rosenstock puts it: "A computer isn't a human being, and it isn't inherently project-based."

High Tech High's early difficulties in using technology to make students more independent learners converged at a long, trying meeting between the school's teachers and administrators and nearly fifty students at the end of the school's first year. It was organized by two students who were giving serious thought to leaving the school because, they said, the school wasn't challenging them academically. Many of the students crowded into the school's conference room complained that they were earning credits for subjects that they hadn't mastered. "I'm spending a lot of time on sea turtles," said one, "but I don't think I'm learning enough biology as a whole." Many wanted High Tech High to become more like traditional high schools, with traditional teaching.

Rosenstock and his colleagues believed strongly in the ability of projects to make demanding academic subjects meaningful to students and to make them more independent, more self-confident learners. And they had seen flashes in High Tech High's first year of the exciting ways in which technology could promote project-based learning. So they set about strengthening rather than scrapping their bold school design in the wake of their students' demands for change. The retraining of their teachers and the other steps they achieved over the next twelve months to make the school's project-based instruction more coherent and more rigorous are a testament both to the level of educators' earnestness in small, autonomous schools, and to the academic dexterity of such schools.

Fittingly, the leaders of the student protest stayed at High Tech High, becoming president and vice president of the school's student body in 2002–03. That year, one applied to Stanford and New York University, the other to Stanford and UCLA.

4 Bond Brokers

The Met, Providence, Rhode Island

Bianca Gray, a deputy policy director to Mayor Vincent Cianci Jr. of Providence, Rhode Island, wasn't a teacher. But she was among the most important people in Tawana Ruiz's high school life.

Tawana (not her real name) recently graduated from the Metropolitan Regional Career and Technical Institute—The Met for short—an alternative public high school in Providence serving mostly troubled students that has taken the radical step of organizing its instruction around internships that its students do with Providence-area professionals. As a junior, she spent two days a week at city hall, where Gray, fifty-four, was her mentor.

Despite its name, The Met isn't a vocational school and

doesn't train students for particular types of work. It requires students to do internships, instead, because the school believes that many students are more motivated and are more successful when they learn through "real world" experiences that they're excited about. No less importantly, the school believes that internships build strong bonds between students and adults, bonds that the school argues are a critical ingredient of successful secondary education.

Many students enter high school alienated, apathetic, and often angry. They simply don't care about school. The Met's response has been to create an education environment where every student is well known to a range of adults during the four years of high school, where students sense that they are cared about, and where they believe their work is valued. Breaking down students' disaffection in this way, The Met believes, is the key to motivating them to learn. The school's motto is "One Student at a Time."

The Met is the culmination of the long and often controversial career of Dennis Littky, fifty-seven, a high school principal and onetime New Hampshire state legislator who has been the subject of two books, a made-for-television movie, and coverage in the *New York Times* and nearly every other major American media outlet.

Littky, who earned doctorates in both psychology and education at the University of Michigan, first introduced features to strengthen bonds between students and adults in the mid-1970s, at a middle school he ran on Long Island, New York. He then expanded them during fourteen years as principal of impoverished Thayer High School in rural Winchester, New Hampshire, a school plagued by fights, truancy, and low test scores before Littky's arrival.

Littky's nontraditional teaching strategies at Thayer—a couple of teachers, for instance, ran a carpentry business with a group of students—and the improvements in student performance that they achieved won national praise. But Littky's strategies were derided by Winchester's conservatives, who wrested control of the local school board and fired Littky, vowing to return Thayer to traditional teaching and "the basics." The New Hampshire courts, however, blocked the firing, Littky's backers recaptured the school board, and in 1993, Littky was named New Hampshire's best principal. By 1996, he and a Thayer colleague, Elliot Washor, had moved to Rhode Island and opened The Met. Today, the school has two hundred students on two campuses, where entering ninth graders are typically three years behind in reading and math.

Littky is a throwback to Progressive educators of nearly a century ago, who wrote that students learn best when confronting challenges that arise in the course of pursuing personal interests. At Thayer, Littky gave every teacher a copy of Progressive John Dewey's treatise "Experience and Education."

Littky adheres to the Progressive belief, pushed by many of Dewey's followers, if not Dewey himself, that no subject is inherently more important than another. "I don't believe that there is any particular subject that we need to know," he says.

That stance leaves Littky outside today's educational mainstream and at odds with the movement in public education to set achievement standards in reading, math, and other core subjects. At Thayer, it led him to use both traditional courses and teaching and unconventional strategies such as the carpentry project.

But at The Met, Littky and Washor have gone further. There are no classrooms at the school. There are no textbooks. There aren't even any teachers.

Instead, there are "advisors," who spend their days working with a group of fourteen students assigned to them as ninth graders and who stay with those students through graduation four years later. They guide the students through a series of internships and independent projects and ensure that they complete the school's learning requirements. It's a highly personalized system. By contrast, teachers in traditional public high schools are responsible for five or six classes and upward of 150 students a day, and every year they get a new group of students.

It was Tawana's advisor, Kristin Hempel, a petite, twenty-six-year-old Swarthmore graduate with a flinty resolve to help her students achieve, who brought Tawana and Bianca Gray together. When I visited The Met she was nearing the end of her third year with Tawana, a tall, outgoing girl with brown eyes, blue nails, and a gold necklace engraved with her name.

It's clear from watching Gray and Hempel work with Tawana and with each other that Littky and Washor are on to something important in providing every student with committed adult advocates—whatever one's views of their progressive curriculum philosophy.

The Met doesn't treat internships lightly. First, students draft "Future Life Journey Maps," in which students discuss what they want their lives to look like in two, five, ten, and twenty-five years. Then they identify internships that would help them achieve their aims. The school sends students out to do oral histories to help them gain insights into the lives and work of people they admire. Met advisors take their students on field trips to such diverse places as air traffic control towers, organic farms, and the Providence courts to stir students' interests. And for the same purpose, the school invites a wide range of guest speakers to morning assemblies to talk about their work.

These steps helped Tawana settle on internships (or LTI's—Learning Through Internships—as the school calls them) that would give the eighteen-year-old an opportunity to help urban teenagers like herself. Typical of The Met's racially diverse, mostly "high risk" students, she had fared poorly as a student before entering The Met, missing a third of her eighth grade year to absenteeism.

Tawana decided she wanted to work in city government, in the hopes of finding a way to help Providence teens. She had worked as a counselor to junior high school students through a previous internship at the Rhode Island Children's Crusade. And in conversations with Hempel and Jill Olson, a former director of volunteers at two Providence-area hospitals who now manages The Met's 220-member mentor network, she hit on the idea of city government as another vehicle for working on behalf of teenagers.

Hempel started to cast around for city hall staffers who might mentor Tawana. Another Met advisor suggested Gray. Hempel brought Tawana to the old city hall building, an eighty-year-old granite edifice with vaulted ceilings, sweeping banisters, and the names of departments stenciled on old oak doors with smoked glass. Tawana sat in Gray's office and quizzed her about her work as the mayor's counselor on youth issues, drawing on the training The Met gives its students in conducting "informational interviews" and "organizational anthropologies" so that students get a clear sense of their mentors' work and thus are less likely to be disappointed once an internship starts. To the same end, Tawana spent a day "shadowing" Gray at work.

Tawana and Gray, a native of Italy, clicked; Tawana wanted to do the internship. Hempel met with the mayoral aide, discussing The Met's educational design and school's expectations for its internships. She also gave Gray the school's video and other training materials on mentoring.

Only then did Hempel officially invite Gray to mentor Tawana. Gray, like the rest of The Met's mentors, agreed to take on the role as an unpaid volunteer. In the last step in the process, The Met had the Providence police do a background check on Gray.

Then Tawana began spending Tuesdays and Thursdays throughout the school year at city hall. At first she spent time learning the rhythm of Gray's job as Mayor Cianci's education aide. She attended staff meetings and press conferences and talked with Cianci's speechwriters and other staffers. Since Met internships are organized around three types of student work—a product for the host organization, research to produce the product, and students' reflections about their research— Tawana then began to help Gray on a study of whether Providence should place adolescent health clinics in the city's schools or elsewhere in the community.

Tawana studied other cities' programs, conducted focus groups of Met students, and sought out the mayor's priorities in a personal interview.

Gray helped at nearly every turn, readying Tawana for her discussion with Cianci, introducing her to focus group experts, even having Spanish speakers in the mayor's office tutor her in Spanish. Tawana spent the other three days of the school week working with Hempel on reading and math.

She also enrolled in a Spanish class at a local community college and under Hempel's guidance wrote a student guide to dealing with relationships, sex, drugs, and other adolescent challenges.

Before long, the relationship that developed between Tawana and Gray extended beyond the substance of their work. As they spent time together in Gray's office, over lunch, and driving together to events at The Met and around the city, Tawana began to trust and confide in the mayoral aide. She would talk about the racism she faced in her daily life, about her absent father, and about how sad she was to read in the newspaper that the father of her friend's child was being sent to prison. To Tawana, Gray was an adult who cared. And that helped erode the apathy toward school that had contributed to her terrible pre-Met attendance record.

Yet the year Gray spent mentoring Tawana represents only one strand of a larger web of relationships that The Met spins around its students to keep them tightly connected to the school and pushing ahead academically.

The school's advisors play a key role in the process. As leaders of "Learning Teams" that The Met establishes for every student they work with mentors and parents to draft individualized quarterly educational plans for students. Then they work to ensure that the plans get executed. A couple of years ago 64 percent of Met parents told the Rhode Island Department of Education that they had spoken with their children's teachers "many times" during the school year, while only 6 percent of the parents of Rhode Island high schoolers as a whole reported that level of teacher contact.

The school's advisors are also in regular contact with their students' mentors. During the two days I spent with Hempel, she met with Tawana and Gray at city hall and with another student and his mentor at a day care center at Rhode Island Hospital. She also kept track (via e-mail) of four students spending a month in Costa Rica studying Spanish and others working at Rhode Island Hospital (as Spanish-language interpreters), at a local stable, at the Providence Zoo, at the city's children's theater company, and at a local bakery.

Hempel was friendly but firm with Tawana at city hall.

"Give me an update on your work," she requested of the teenager, as they sat side by side in Gray's office, Hempel taking notes on a keyboard attached to a Palm Pilot as Tawana narrated.

When Tawana responded that she hadn't been able to find much about Milwaukee's teen health clinics on the Internet, Hempel straightened in her chair. Gray urged Tawana to "use the telephone." She also suggested that the Council on Mental Health "has a lot of data" that would be germane to Tawana's project. And she urged the student to contact members of a mayoral Council on Drug Abuse.

"OK," Hempel said, typing rapidly. "Here are the things you are going to do in the next couple of days: draft your focus group questions, call Milwaukee, and read Kids Count," she said, helping Tawana prioritize her work.

Tawana pledged to do the work. But Hempel continued to cajole Tawana. After leaving Gray's office we had lunch at a nearby deli. "Let's follow up on today's meeting with Bianca, at school, tomorrow, at 11:00," Hempel suggested between banter about haircuts and a recent movie outing the two of them had with Tawana's younger sister.

Hempel's persistence is typical at The Met. And given that many of the school's entering students lack self-discipline and a sense that school's important, it's frequently necessary. But there wouldn't be enough hours in the day for teachers in traditional high schools to encourage their many students with the frequency that Hempel does. The organization of traditional high schools, in fact, makes it difficult for many teachers merely to know their students' names.

Nearly every element of The Met's educational design, in contrast, seems to strengthen the school's message to students that they and the work they do are important. Oral exams are a big part of the way The Met measures student performance, partly because they build students' speaking skills and self-confidence, but also because they signal to students that the school community cares about what they have to say. It's not uncommon to have as many as three dozen students and advisors in attendance at the "exhibitions" that every Met student delivers four times a year.

Toward the same end, every graduating senior delivers a valedictory address in the final week of school, the school has replaced report cards with detailed narratives of student progress, students are given a role in drafting and enforcing the school's discipline code, and advisors are expected to take trips with their students once or twice a year (shortly after I visited the school Hempel and her advisees went camping together on the Rhode Island coast).

In reaching out to students in these ways The Met has flouted the traditional prohibition in public education against teacher involvement in students' personal lives. In a particularly striking example, Littky has required students since his Thayer days to write regularly in journals about what they are learning, their internships, and other subjects. Advisors read the students' work, both to improve students' writing and to signal to them, again, that adults are interested in what they're thinking. Littky's critics attacked the practice in New Hampshire, charging that Thayer teachers were prying into students' private lives. But The Met's advisors believe that it's simply the school's job to help students with problems that surface through journals or in other ways. "A lot of stuff gets in the way of learning," says Littky. "We can't pretend it doesn't."

To help students stay out of trouble during summer vacations, for example, The Met raises funds for them to travel or work outside of Providence. Met students have been camp counselors in Pennsylvania, house builders in Honduras, and Outward Bound participants in Utah. Last year, the school's parent newsletter announced that, "The families of two Met students are in crisis. If any family would consider taking in these students, please call Jill or Anita in the main office." Within a week, two other Met households had volunteered to take in the needy students.

The size of The Met contributes to its strong sense of community. In sharp contrast to traditional public high schools of one thousand students or more, schools where anonymity is often pervasive, The Met's enrollment of only two hundred is split between two locations. One's on the fourth floor of a renovated downtown department store. The other's in Providence's gritty West End, next door to a Providence Fire Department training facility. It's a single story, square structure that has the look of a community center lacking athletic facilities (there are none at The Met). That's what Littky had in mind. "I wanted it small enough so that it didn't seem like a school," he says.

The whole student body can assemble in the building's common area, and does, every morning, for what's called a Pick-Me-Up, an admixture of announcements, performances, and presentations. A local string quartet has performed at Pick-Me-Up. A Met parent has talked to students about her career as a corrections officer.

The day I was there an advisor delivered a pep talk. "You have to believe in yourselves," she declared as she walked the room with a wireless microphone. Later, as Charlie Plant, the campus principal, was making announcements, a student walked into the building. Plant called her up to where he was standing and, at his urging, the gathering sang "Happy Birthday" to the blushing sixteen-year-old sporting super baggy pants and lots of earrings.

Then Plant turned the mike over to a student who made a scheduled presentation to the fifty or so students and teachers present on her senior thesis, a project about racism in Providence.

"I want you to be strong and independent," she told her audience. "I don't want you to go through what I've been through," she said, recounting a troubling racial incident that she had endured. Later, she answer questions from the assembled students.

The Met promotes public discourse, says Littky, because it builds speaking skills and self-confidence, but also because it engenders trust among the school's students and connects them to the school community. If students fight or are suspended they must discuss their transgressions in a Pick-Me-Up presentation.

What was particularly striking about the Pick-Me-Up I attended was the casual but pervasive air of respect that students demonstrated toward one another. The Met, it seems, treats students in adultlike ways, and students respond with adultlike levels of maturity.

Littky and Washor also work hard to forge strong bonds

between their teachers, believing that they are the foundation of the school's powerful sense of community. Every Met teacher plays an active role in selecting new staff members. And Littky and Washor have extended the staff's school year ten days beyond that of the school's students, in order to hold staff retreats. They also pay teachers extra to attend two weeks of Met-run summer workshops.

They aren't exclusively working sessions. Once, Littky and Washor brought along a masseuse, treating everyone to a fifteen-minute massage. "Somebody's got to buy the pizzas, bring in the birthday balloons, spice up faculty meetings with fancy pastry and lousy jokes," says Littky, who, a stocky five-foot-ten and fond of blue jeans, sports a big gray goatee, wire-rimmed glasses, and curly hair that fluffs out under an African skull cap that he often wears. "What a school is depends more on how people treat each other than on anything else." To Littky, the key is an atmosphere of conviviality, "where people are known and valued for who they are, not just for the work they do."

The Met's faculty is, as a result, tight-knit and highly loyal to the school's students. In a nod to traditionalist teaching, Littky and Washor permit students to take courses at local colleges. When Tawana struggled in a community college anatomy class that she had worked into her schedule, Hempel had the student over to her house on Saturdays to study. The school's staff takes students on tours of college campuses. And lest there's any doubt about the school's valuation of its students, The Met holds its graduations in a stately, ivy-covered building at nearby Brown University.

There are plenty of challenges to creating the degree of advocacy for students that's present at The Met.

Even with an intern director and a large network of mentors it's often difficult to place students in productive internships. There have been instances where half the students in an advisory haven't been placed in internships until the middle of the school year. In response, the school last year began having incoming ninth graders go to "summer camp," where they get a head start on launching their internships.

The Met also struggles to teach traditional academic skills through its internships (Met students must take Rhode Island's graduation tests in reading and math).

It doesn't lack for a plan to help students acquire such skills. Each LTI in theory moves students closer to achieving the school's "learning goals" in five areas: "communications" (where the learning goals range from studying a second language to writing clearly); "social reasoning" (resolving conflicts, participating in civic activities); "empirical reasoning" (testing hypotheses, interpreting data); "quantitative reasoning" (arithmetic, algebra, estimation, number sense); and "personal qualities" (respecting one's self and others; managing time effectively). Met advisors weave tasks to achieve the learning goals into students' quarterly learning contracts, end-of-year exhibitions, and graduation projects.

And the school is successful in using internships as the cornerstones of this work. Eliot Levine, the author of *One Kid at a Time,* a book about The Met, recounts how a largely unengaged student's interest in hairstyles and a beauty parlor internship led to her reading the story of C. J. Walker, a wealthy African American entrepreneur and civil rights activist who made her money in hair care products—a story that prompted the student to enter an essay contest on the civil rights movement and then, after she won the contest, to travel with her advisor to Little Rock, Arkansas, to explore the history of school desegregation. The student went on to do projects at The Met on diabetes and domestic violence. "I went from hair care to human repair," she remarked in her "valedictorian" address.

But at times the enormous energy that The Met's mentors and advisors expend on students isn't rewarded— at least not by traditional academic measures. Despite Hempel's and Gray's efforts to motivate Tawana, she let her project on teen clinics languish, focusing instead on her twenty-hour-a-week job at McDonald's and becoming preoccupied with buying the right clothes for a school prom. She made her year-end presentation, but it was, to Gray, perfunctory.

"The lack of sophistication of student work," Littky acknowledges, "is a challenge."

Some skills, moreover, including "empirical reasoning" (the scientific method) and particularly "quantitative reasoning" (math), are tough to teach through internships even if students are enthusiastic. "We haven't been able to make math work for enough students," says Littky. "We aren't doing it very well." The Met students who have ex-celled in mathematics have done so in traditional ways: I met a senior at the school named David Greenberg who was interning as a software developer and hardware technician at a local computer company while taking advanced math courses at Brown University.

It's also the case that Littky and his colleagues could never have created such an extraordinarily student-centered school if they hadn't freed themselves from many traditional school system strictures.

The Met is a state-funded regional institution that is largely independent of the Providence public school system. And it was created from scratch with powerful backers such as Ted Sizer, the influential school reformer then based at Brown University, Peter McWalter, Rhode Island's reform-minded education commissioner, and Stanley Goldstein, the then-CEO of CVS Pharmacy, the state's largest corporation.

As a result, the Rhode Island legislature has given Littky

and Washor the authority to hire teachers who share The Met's educational philosophy instead of having to take whoever happens to be at the top of the Providence schools' seniority list. They have been able to create a high school without coaches or band instructors or assistant principals, allowing The Met to afford the school's fourteen-to-one student/advisor ratio. And they have been able to sidestep state course requirements that would have quashed the school's internships and union work rules that would have blocked its longer school year for teachers.

And because The Met was a new school, Littky and Washor didn't have to win over a building full of traditional teachers to their one-kid-at-a-time philosophy.

That's key, because The Met simply wouldn't work without teachers who are as dedicated as Hempel to the school's philosophy. Juggling the highly idiosyncratic studies of fourteen students day after day is demanding work, requiring Met advisors to learn new subjects quickly, be highly organized, and spend long hours with often trying students. During my visit Hempel ended a ten-hour stint at school by climbing into her car at 5:00 P.M. and driving forty-five minutes to discuss school work with an advisee who had checked himself into a drug treatment center. Hempel says that The Met's "relentless intimacy," in particular, is "draining," the "best but hardest" part of working at the school. Like Hempel, the school's dozen or so other advisors tend to be young, bright, and idealistic.

But the relationships that The Met engenders between students and adults have created a school culture that stands in stark contrast to that of the nation's predominantly large, impersonal public high schools.

West Providence isn't a safe place at night. But The Met's campus has no fences and no bars on its windows—and no vandalism. Nearly 90 percent of Met parents report to Rhode Island education authorities that the school is "a safe place."

Students' strong sense of belonging at The Met has produced average daily student attendance rates of 93 percent, sharply higher than the 80 percent average rate at Providence's other public high schools. And of the 241 students enrolled at The Met during the school's first four years only 8 percent dropped out. The city's other high schools lost an average of 27 percent of their students during the same period. "They start taking themselves more seriously because they are taken seriously," says Washor of his students.

And if The Met doesn't routinely turn out students with test scores that match those of students in affluent suburban high schools, it nonetheless makes substantial academic strides with students who frequently enter The Met, as Littky puts it, "with lots of baggage." Every one of the ninety-three students in the school's first two graduating classes has been admitted to at least one postsecondary school, and collectively they have won $800,000 in scholarships to places ranging from the Community College of Rhode Island to the University of Rhode Island and private institutions like Marlboro College in Vermont, where Tawana is now a freshman, Curry College, and, in two instances, Brown University. The truth is that many of them probably wouldn't have finished high school if they hadn't gone to The Met.

"My survival mantra," says Littky, "is, 'Compared to what?'" Compared to where they are when they enter the school, he says, Met students "move a long way."

Given the troubling anonymity that pervades the nation's traditional high schools, there are surely many students more affluent than The Met's whose high school educations would also be greatly strengthened by relationships with mentors like Bianca Gray and teachers like Kristin Hempel.

5 Ownership Stakes

Minnesota
New Country School,
Henderson, Minnesota

One wouldn't think a group of teachers seated around a table in the library of a rural Minnesota high school would be a revolutionary event in public education. Yet when Keven Kroehler and the rest of the staff of the Minnesota New Country School got together after school one day they were taking part in a bold experiment to strengthen the public school teaching profession by reshaping the governance of public high schools.

They had gathered as members of EdVisions, a "teacher cooperative" that New Country's board of directors had hired to run the public charter school. Public school teachers have traditionally been salaried school system employees. And since the rise of industrial-style teacher unionism in the early 1960s the roles and responsibilities of teachers and principals and other administrators have been strictly separated. Teachers have been labor, administrators have been management. And it has been management's job, and management's alone, to run schools—to select teaching strategies, hire and fire staff, draft budgets, and shape the way the school day is organized.

But the New Country teachers in the EdVisions co-op play very different roles than those that public education has scripted for teachers in recent decades. They share in the ownership of the business that the school board has contracted with to run New Country, and thus they are responsible for drafting the school's educational plan and executing it successfully. When the school was being organized, they set spending priorities, selected teaching strategies, and staffed the school. When New Country's teachers had spent an hour talking with Kroehler about his strengths and weaknesses and another teacher joked good-naturedly, "Well, should we vote him off the island?" Kroehler, a respected senior teacher, smiled, but weakly: EdVisions, he knew, would factor the results of the session into its decision whether to renew his contract for the next school year.

EdVisions is a new model of school governance designed to nurture the spirit of professionalism among teachers and strengthen the performance of public high schools by increasing teachers' stake in the success of their schools in a very literal way.

Teaching has struggled to attract the best and brightest college graduates in the several decades since law, medicine, and other professions started to draw talented women and African Americans away from teaching, which had long served as a haven for women and blacks excluded from the legal and medical professions. Industrial-style unionism exacerbated the problem by imposing lock-step salary schedules and strict labor-management roles on school staffs, making it difficult for able and ambitious teachers to take on new roles and responsibilities in schools without becoming administrators.

EdVisions has countered these conditions by affording small teams of teachers opportunities to run schools and to reap rewards when they do so successfully. It has extended to teaching the professionalism and the entrepreneurialism of law firms and medical practices. And it has created a powerful antidote to the isolating teaching environments of many large, comprehensive high schools. Having both the authority and responsibility to make their schools successful and working in small schools, which makes staffwide collaboration possible, EdVisions teachers like those at New Country work together and work hard to make their schools productive places of learning.

Today EdVisions runs New Country and nine other Minnesota charter schools—publicly funded schools that function independently of traditional school boards and teacher unions—out of a pine-paneled storefront office in tiny Henderson, Minnesota, a rural hamlet in the flood-plain of the Minnesota River about sixty miles southwest of Minneapolis.

The organization was founded in the mid-1990s by a local Henderson group led by Doug Thomas, a member of the Le Sueur-Henderson school board who had been help-ing several area teachers establish a new school under Min-nesota's 1991 charter statute. Thomas worked at the time as a regional representative of the Center for School Change at the University of Minnesota's Humphrey Institute of Public Affairs. And through the center's director, Joe Nathan, he got to know Ted Kolderie, a writer and education gadfly who had been one of the driving forces behind the passage of Minne-sota's first-in-the-nation charter school law.

Kolderie and other local reformers had hit on the idea of "teacher ownership" as a way of unshackling educators from what they believed was the debilitating bureaucracy of public education. As with charter schools, they argued, giv-ing teachers a proprietor's stake in their schools' success would increase productivity and lead to greater innovation in public education—the same thinking that lies behind two other recent strands of school reform: "site-based man-agement," an attempt to push greater authority down to the school level; and, more dramatically, the rise of such companies as Edison Schools, Inc., which manages public schools for profit and offers its school staffs stock options.

Kolderie and the others were drawn to the co-op concept

because of Minnesota's long tradition of feed store, dairy, and other agricultural cooperatives. But teachers, they suggested, could also organize themselves into partnerships, corporations, and other legal entities, both for-profit and nonprofit, and they could contract with traditional public schools and school boards as well as charter schools. A partnership of top science teachers, Kolderie suggested by way of example, might market themselves to rural school systems that traditionally struggle to staff their high school science courses.

Thomas was taken with Kolderie's ideas, and when the Le Sueur-Henderson school board granted the local teachers a charter to start a new school in late 1993, he encouraged them to set up what would be the nation's first teacher cooperative. With the help of a St. Paul attorney specializing in co-op law, Dan Mott, they did. And the school's board of directors hired the fledgling organization to run the charter school—Minnesota New Country.

Each teacher in the EdVisions schools with a year's work in the schools can become an equal voting co-op member simply by paying one hundred dollars for a single share of stock. And though EdVisions as an organization is legally responsible for the schools' performance, the co-op relies heavily on members at each site to manage the schools. Among Keven Kroehler's interviewers at New Country, for instance, were the school's three-person staffing committee. They would later recommend to the EdVisions board of directors—a fourteen-member group that consists of two teachers from each EdVisions school and two at-large members—that Kroehler be rehired.

New Country has ten full-time teachers, who educate some 120 students in grades seven through twelve in Henderson, in a building that backs up to the levee protecting the town from the Minnesota River. The students come from many different school systems in the region, where many of them had struggled with their school work and with their peers.

True to Kolderie's prediction, EdVisions has designed an innovative education at New Country for the school's challenging students. As if creating something of a modern-day one-room schoolhouse, they've organized the bulk of New Country's seventeen-thousand-square-foot building into a single open space that houses individual student and teacher workstations; the only appendages are a science classroom, a greenhouse, a library room, and a woodworking/auto shop.

There are no bells, no hallways, no homerooms, and few traditional, teacher-led courses at New Country. Instead, drawing on the educational philosophy of John Dewey, teachers (or advisors, as they're called at the school) help students do independent and group projects during the school year, ranging from boat-building to raising angora goats as part of a student-run weaving business. Several years ago the school attracted national television attention for students' research into the causes of deformities in local frogs.

Many other things also set New Country apart from traditional high schools: the absence of a principal (replaced by a teacher leadership team); a schoolwide daily silent reading period; the absence of an extensive sports program and other costly staples of large, comprehensive high schools (which have led to New Country's favorable student-to-teacher ratio); a calendar that has students at the school for five weeks and then off for a week, year-round, with the exception of a two-week break in August; students rather than janitors cleaning the school daily; the school's giving every student an e-mail account to help them stay in touch with teachers.

But in exchange for the privilege of designing their schools, EdVisions teachers must do much more than simply teach. "You are forced to look at a lot of other issues," says Kroehler, who, for a twenty-five-hundred-dollar stipend, handles New Country's purchasing, financial reporting, and accounting. "In Colorado [where he taught for over a decade] the principal would get people in the room and say you've got three hundred dollars to divide up. We weren't responsible for anything significant in the budget. Here, we're responsible for the whole thing [$1 million]."

They are also responsible for a host of other tasks that

teachers typically don't do, including staffing, student discipline, maintenance, and even marketing. New Country lead teacher Dee Thomas found herself handing out New Country flyers at a stand at the Le Sueur Farm and Home Show, a big regional gathering held every year in a hockey rink at the Le Sueur civic center. Because EdVisions has a contract to run New Country, says Thomas, "It's not someone else's fault if something doesn't work, and it's not up to someone else to fix the problem."

Perhaps surprisingly, that's a situation that New Country teachers like. "The majority of public school teachers are locked into a static, repetitive schedule every day," says Doug Thomas. "At New Country, it's as if they are running a small consulting business—constantly working with each other and with their customers to solve problems. It's liberating for many teachers." Many experiments in site-based management have sought to energize educators in this way in recent years, but the bulk of them have failed to do so because teachers and principals typically have been given only token amounts of decision-making authority.

Another consequence of the new roles for teachers is a strong sense of mutual responsibility among New Country's staff—a quality that's lacking in many traditional public schools. Several days before I visited New Country, the staff met for three hours on a Saturday to debate the plight of a student who hadn't met the school's graduation requirements. She'd been admitted to a postsecondary vocational program but she needed New Country's approval before she could receive the financial aid that she needed to attended the program. Only one of New Country's teachers didn't attend the Saturday session—because his wife was working and a child was sick in bed.

What's driving many New Country teachers to work so hard on the school's behalf is in part the same thing that drives every entrepreneurial enterprise—pursuit of a service that sells. "If we don't attract kids, there's no money to fund our contract," says Kroehler. "Everything we do has to be for the good of the school."

It is that reality of the marketplace that has led New Country's teachers to give students individualized attention through such things as hour-long student-parent-teacher meetings several times a year. It is why the New Country staff gather every summer to address the school's weaknesses (with parents and students invited to share their perspectives). It is why New Country's leadership team sponsors workshops on teaching strategies and other topics for the school's teachers every Thursday afternoon.

And it is one reason why EdVisions did not retain the teacher who followed Kroehler on the agenda in the New Country library during my visit. Each spring students submit the names of three teachers that they would like to have as advisors the following school year. Then they are assigned to the advisory group of their first-, second-, or third-choice teacher. Teachers' contracts are jeopardized when teachers fail to attract sufficient numbers of students to their advisories, says Dee Thomas, who was the principal of a traditional Minnesota high school before becoming a New Country teacher. EdVisions released Kroehler's colleague in part because his advisory had shrunk to eight students. Nor is New Country's advisor-selection system a popularity contest, Thomas notes. Most students select teachers who they sense are going to help them academically. Needless to say, students do not often get lost in such an environment.

Because New Country's teachers are responsible for the school's educational experience, they tend to have the same educational philosophy. The school, as a result, has a clear sense of what it is trying to do with its students—a key ingredient of successful schools.

At New Country teachers have embraced the concept of having students learn independently through projects, a teaching strategy that requires very different roles for teachers. They don't lecture on specific subjects in classrooms the way traditional high school teachers do. The desks of each teacher and the dozen or more students in the teacher's advisory group are clustered together in a section of New Country's large, open space. The bulk of teachers' time is spent helping students complete projects in a range of subjects, in a role closer to that of a coach than a conventional teacher. And the relationship between students and teachers at New Country is decidedly informal. "Hey, Keven, I need some help," a sandy-haired sophomore called from his desk as I talked with Kroehler at the school. Kroehler walked over to the student, who had a chess game on his computer screen. He gave the student the advice he sought and then moved on to work with two students who were teaching themselves physics out of a textbook.

New Country's staff works hard to recruit teachers who buy into the school's progressive philosophy. Special education teacher Jeff Anderson says that nearly the entire staff at New Country interviewed him when he came to the school last year after nine years in the Minneapolis public school system. "There was also a different feel to the interviews," he says. "People were talking about my educational beliefs, wanting to know if they were in line with the school's."

During the lunch hour one day I found Dee Thomas huddled over sandwiches with teacher Dean Lind, a lanky former farmer and agriculture instructor who serves as EdVisions' treasurer. They were talking through the details of a plan to have a New Country teacher mentor the school's new students, as a way of helping them catch on to New Country's system of independent projects. There was also a lot of talk among New Country's teachers when I was there about a proposal Lind had made recently to make the school's salary system more meritocratic: a performance-

based pay scale that would tie half of teachers' pay to performance in ten areas, including teaching ability, work
ethic, and parent relations. Such discussions reflect another
quality of teacher ownership and small size: faster, more
nimble responses to schools' needs. Says Dee Thomas: "In
other schools that I've been in the bureaucracy smothers
teachers' great ideas; here, we don't have to go through subcommittees of subcommittees to get things done."

The benefits to New Country of this minimal bureaucracy can be found throughout the school. Originally the
school subcontracted its purchasing, accounting, and fi-
nance work to outside firms. Now Kroehler is doing those
tasks because the school's teachers saw that the subcon-
tracting results weren't great, and they were able to act on
their insights. "We realized that we were doing most of the
work anyway," says Kroehler. "Now it doesn't take two weeks
to get purchase orders filled and we know that what gets
ordered is needed."

EdVisions hasn't been a budget-busting expense.
Though at New Country the average teacher salary is nearly
15 percent above the Minnesota average, personnel costs are
only 57 percent of the school's budget, sharply lower than
the statewide average of nearly 80 percent. That's because
the New Country school design eliminates many traditional
staff roles. In addition to doing without a principal, New
Country has no custodians, no cafeteria workers, no deans,

and no full-time coaches. The fact that the New Country's teachers can—and do—move backward as well as forward on the school's pay scale, something that's unheard of under traditional public school pay scales, also lowers salary costs slightly. Taken together, such measures helped New Country's board achieve a 20 percent budget surplus in 2001–02, money that the school spent on technology upgrades, teacher training, and higher teacher salaries, all with a lower student-to-teacher ratio than is found in most public high schools.

Though EdVisions is set up as a for-profit entity, the co-op has not built profit margins into its contracts and so far higher teacher salaries have been members' only "dividends." But the co-op has begun charging its schools consulting fees for having its members do such things as technology installations and accounting work, and it has begun marketing its curriculum. As a result, Doug Thomas says EdVisions may soon distribute its first dividend checks. In the end, though, it seems to be the chance to be in charge and the challenge of attracting students that motivates New Country's teachers, not the prospect of profits.

Teacher ownership, of course, doesn't suit every teacher. Some aren't prepared to do the substantial amount of additional work that running schools requires. And some don't like the responsibility it entails. They'd rather teach in traditional public schools, where there's less autonomy but also less accountability. Some teachers, even good ones, carve out quiet niches in large schools, where they are not bothered from year to year and they don't bother others. They might find New Country—with its collegial oversight and requirement that every teacher take an interest in the work of every other—draining, even intrusive. But for many teachers these same prospects can be energizing.

The risks are real for EdVisions teachers, as they discovered in the summer of 2001, after former staff at one of the co-op's schools filed for state unemployment benefits. Because the teachers work for EdVisions, under Minnesota law the ten-school co-op collectively and the EdVisions teachers individually face the potential of higher unemployment-insurance premiums, eventually totaling over two hundred thousand dollars a year for the entire EdVisions membership in the wake of the claims. "It was a shocker to many EdVisions members," says Doug Thomas.

In response, Thomas and EdVisions' other leaders have moved quickly to reduce the schools' collective legal liability. They are establishing separate, legally autonomous co-ops at each school they serve and are transforming EdVisions into an umbrella organization with the narrower role of supplying teacher training and other services to its members' schools.

Ironically, Thomas and other EdVisions leaders have struggled to get many EdVisions teachers to grasp the urgency of the unemployment-insurance rate hike because the co-op had turned over so much authority to the teachers in the schools it runs that it has been difficult for many teachers to recognize the co-op's role in their professional lives. To a number of New Country teachers, EdVisions has been merely "a payroll service," says Kroehler, a perception that has been encouraged by the fact that New Country teachers who aren't voting members of EdVisions have been given a role in running the school alongside EdVisions stockholders. To enhance EdVisions' stature in teachers' eyes, treasurer Dean Lind has urged that the EdVisions board of directors be given the final say on staffing and other major issues in co-op schools, an unlikely step now that the organization is subdividing into a confederation of co-ops. Lind also has proposed that only teachers owning shares in the co-op be permitted to vote within school-level committees.

Ultimately, there's a need to test more models of teacher ownership, particularly those where teacher-owners are working for traditional public schools and school systems. Because charter schools function independently of school systems and are thus largely self-managing, New Country's status as a charter and EdVisions' presence in the school both contribute to the entrepreneurial esprit de corps among the school's teachers. As does the fact that Minnesota's charter school law requires a plurality of teachers on charter school boards. EdVisions-like experiments in traditional public schools would both test the strength of teacher ownership as a school reform and greatly extend the reform's reach.

There's likely to be strong resistance from public school bureaucracies reluctant to relinquish their influence over schools and from teacher unions troubled by teachers losing job protections. Collective-bargaining contracts would effectively give teacher unions veto power over teacher-ownership proposals.

But Ron Newell, a former college professor and co-founder of EdVisions, says the aim of teacher ownership "isn't to break unions, but to push professionalism to the forefront of teacher organizations." And that's something that teacher unions are increasingly interested in. "Young people coming into teaching are insisting on a strong professional culture, they have a more entrepreneurial spirit and are less trustful of traditional public institutions," says Louise Sundin, the president of the Minneapolis Federation of Teachers and a vice president of the American Federation of Teachers. The working lives of teachers at New Country suggest that teacher ownership in small learning communities like New Country is a promising route to the professionalism that Sundin is talking about.

Epilogue

Scaling Up

High Tech High, The Met, New Country, Julia Richman, and Urban Academy are a collective expression of a promising new vision of the American high school, one that is capable of delivering a rigorous academic education to a majority of students.

The challenge is to introduce the schools' programs throughout the public education system, to take the models to scale. If we truly want to transform our system of secondary education we cannot rely on the extraordinary efforts to transform individual schools. We can't rely on what one commentator calls "random acts of innovation and heroic leadership." Instead, we have to identify the fundamental changes that have to be made in the education system in order to introduce an alternative to the comprehensive high school on a large scale.

The successful creation of the Julia Richman Educational Complex argues for creating new, small schools from scratch, either as free-standing institutions or as a group of autonomous schools under a single roof. The centralizing tendencies of curriculum departments and other organizational structures in large, comprehensive high schools make it very difficult to create the sense of ownership and shared identity that are such important ingredients of successful schools. Simply breaking large schools into houses and other subunits often leaves such structural problems in place.

Part of the solution here, particularly in urban school systems, is to locate small schools of several hundred students in office buildings and other spaces that are more readily available than new school buildings and less expensive to procure. A network of such schools could share centrally located sports, music, and performing arts facilities.

Ensuring that these new-style schools have distinctive and focused educational programs is critical. School systems have to resist the temptation to try to deliver every type of educational service in a single school. If they don't, their chances of establishing a strong sense of community are much diminished. Instead, school systems should respond to students' diverse needs and interests through a

wide range of independent programs. If towns want to create big marching bands and powerhouse sports teams, let
them do so with students from several small, independently
run schools. The point is that there are ways around the collective and idealized remembrances of high school "as we
knew it."

It's far easier to maintain a school's distinctiveness and
sense of community when its students and teachers are
permitted to select their schools. There's less pressure to
expand a school's mission when its key constituents have
chosen to be part of the school community. They tend to be
loyal to the school's mission rather than want to change
it. And as the educator Deborah Meier has written, "Good
schools thrive on the eager and passionate loyalty of their
members."

Another critical ingredient of coherent, tightly knit
schools is autonomy—the freedom to hire and fire staff,
shape budgets, and set instructional strategies. As the experience of the EdVisions teacher cooperative at New Country
suggests, building a distinctive educational vision is far easier when the school is able to hire teachers who share the
vision and when it's able to deploy its resources and tai-
lor its teaching to support its chosen strategies. As the
EdVisions teachers also demonstrated, when schools are
put in charge of their own fate, the educators in them are
more than willing to work hard and be held accountable for

their performance. Giving teachers ownership stakes in small learning communities is a valuable strategy for attracting the best and the brightest into the teaching profession and keeping them there.

Many state and federal regulations undercut schools' autonomy. In some instances, state and federal programs operate in high schools independently of the schools' principals, who have no role in the programs' staffing or budgeting. Similarly, rigid, externally imposed funding formulas make it difficult for schools to forge unique identities.

So do many teacher-union contracts. Traditional union-bargained rules make the sorts of roles that teachers play at The Met, New Country, and Julia Richman difficult if not impossible to introduce elsewhere. Seniority-based hiring systems, which give teachers with the most years of service the first shot at job openings regardless of whether they're the strongest candidates or embrace a school's educational philosophy, undercut the sense of community and the level of loyalty in many high schools. The new American high school requires enlightened union leadership of the sort that the United Federation of Teachers displayed during the creation of the Julia Richman Education Complex. Unless they are able to select their own staff and manage their resources themselves, small schools are likely to function no differently than large schools.

In effect, as Tom Vander Ark of the Gates Foundation has

argued, we need comprehensive school systems, not comprehensive schools. We need many different types of high schools, each distinctive, each with a strong sense of identity. And school systems need to permit students and teachers to select from among them.

But creating such a system of schools isn't enough. Schools, ultimately, have to educate students and educate them well. In the words of Michelle Fine, a New York University professor and an advocate of small high schools, "Small . . . will produce a sense of belonging almost immediately, but hugging is not the same as algebra. Rigor and care must be braided together, or we run the risk of creating small, nurturing environments that aren't schools." Keeping kids connected to schools and schooling is critical, but ultimately it's merely a means to a larger end—high standards of student achievement. Ultimately, the first priority of every high school must be to stretch students academically to prepare them for the academic rigors of college.

To be sure, that's a daunting challenge for a school like The Met. Many of its students arrive completely unprepared to handle rigorous academic work and it would be unrealistic to expect the school to place every graduate in the Ivy League. But the Met and Urban Academy have demonstrated that redesigned high schools are able to produce impressive academic results with students who have performed poorly in comprehensive high schools.

That is not to say, of course, that small, personalized high schools are only suited to struggling students, or that comprehensive high schools ill-serve every student. Today's comprehensive high schools educate perhaps a third of their students well. But about half of their students graduate ill-prepared for the rigors of college work, and another fifth do not graduate at all. That is just not good enough anymore.

High schools in Denmark called "technical gymnasiums" teach us that the project-based learning that schools like High Tech High have used to draw reluctant students into academic studies can take place on a wide scale and can be as demanding as any traditional teaching.

Throughout the Scandinavian nation students in technical gymnasium schools prepare for national tests known as the Higher Technical Examinations (HTX) in a two- or three-year course that focuses on students solving problems and doing a series of rigorous individual and group projects as varied as mapping the North Sea and building dog sleds. Danish universities consider the HTX exams to be no less academically demanding than those taken by students in the country's academic high schools.

The key to the model's success, Danish educators say, is that the technical projects are designed specifically to teach the challenging skills on the national HTX examinations, which students in turn must pass to enter a wide range of vocations.

Planning and launching the thousands of small high schools that it would take to replace the nation's large, comprehensive secondary schools would require a substantial investment. But it wouldn't be necessary to sustain the increased spending once the new schools were up and running. The Met, High Tech High, Urban Academy, and New Country have demonstrated that small schools can be highly efficient educational institutions.

The schools have also demonstrated that rigid standardized testing regimes of the sort that are in increasingly wide use in this country aren't always the best way to achieve the high academic standards that we want for high school students today. If schools like Urban are able to get the vast majority of their students into college using Inquiry Learning and project-based proficiencies, then they shouldn't be put in a position by state testing edicts of having to sacrifice those successful strategies.

The prospect of high schools on a more human scale ultimately requires a belief on the part of educators and policymakers that the necessary changes to the status quo needed to create such high schools are worth the hard work needed to achieve them. The stories of the students and educators at Urban Academy, The Met, New Country, Julia Richman, and High Tech High suggest emphatically that they are.

Appendix

Model High Schools Nationwide

Contact information for Urban Academy, High Tech High, The Met, and New Country is listed below. Also included are the names and addresses of other high schools nationwide that break sharply with the traditions of the comprehensive high school. They are small, personalized schools with high academic expectations, a strong sense of community, and a clear set of educational beliefs that shape their course offerings, their teaching strategies, and much else about the schools.

*The Metropolitan Regional Career
and Technical Center (The Met)*
80 Washington Street
Providence, RI 02903
(401) 277-5046
www.metcenter.org

*Urban Academy Laboratory High School
(at Julia Richmond Education Complex)*
317 E. 67th Street
New York, NY 10021
(212) 570-5284
www.urbanacademy.org

Minnesota New Country School (MNCS)
P.O. Box 488
210 Main Street
Henderson, MN 56044
(507) 248-3353
www.mncs.k12.mn.us

The Gary and Jerri Jacobs High Tech High
2861 Womble Road
San Diego, CA 92106
(619) 243-5000
www.hightechhigh.org/index.shtml

Other small, personalized high schools by region:

Northeast

Boston Arts Academy
174 Ipswich Street
Boston, MA 02215
(617) 635.6470
artsacad.boston.k12.ma.us

Fenway High School
174 Ipswich Street
Boston, MA 22215
(617) 635-9911
fenway.boston.k12.ma.us

Frederick Douglass Academy
2581 Adam Clayton Powell Boulevard
New York, NY 10039
(212) 491-4107

Mission Hill School
67 Alleghany
Boston, MA 02120
(617) 635-6384
www.missionhillschool.org

Southeast

Ben Franklin Academy
1585 Clifton Road, N.E.
Atlanta, GA 30329
(404) 633-7404
www.benfranklinacademy.org

Benjamin Banneker Academic High School
800 Euclid Street, N.W.
Washington, DC 20001
(202) 673-7322
www.benjaminbanneker.net

Maya Angelou Public Charter School
1851 9th Street, N.W.
Washington, DC 20001
(202) 939-9080
www.seeforever.org/MAPCS

Midwest

Amelia High School
1351 Clough Pike
Batavia, OH 45103-2546
(513) 753-5120
www.westcler.org/ah

Catherine Ferguson Academy
2750 Selden Avenue
Detroit, MI 48208
(313) 596-4766

Glen Este High School
4342 Glen Este-Withamsville Road
Cincinnati, OH 45245-1599
(513) 943-8211
www.westcler.org/GH

Noble Street Charter High School
1012 N. Noble
Chicago, IL 60622
(773) 862-1449
www.cps.k12.il.us/Schools/Opportunities/Charter/School_
Profiles/Noble_Street/noble_street.html

Perspectives Charter School
1532 South Michigan Avenue
Chicago, IL 60605
(312) 431-8770
www.perspectivescs.org

School of Environmental Studies at the Minnesota Zoo
12155 Johnny Cake Ridge Road
Apple Valley, MN 55124
(952) 431-8750
www.isd196.k12.mn.us/ses

Wyandotte High School
25th & Minnesota Avenue
Kansas City, KS 66102
(913) 627-7650
home.sprintmail.com/~pelliso01/Wyandotte.html

Northwest

The Center School at Seattle Center
305 Harrison Street
Seattle, WA 98109
(206) 956-3235
www.orgsites.com/wa/thecenterschool

Chugach School District
9312 Vanguard Drive, #100
Anchorage, AK 99507
(907) 522-7400
www.chugachschools.com

Nathan Hale High School
10750 30th Avenue, N.E.
Seattle, WA 98125
(206) 252-3680
hale.ssd.k12.wa.us

Tacoma School of the Arts
601 South 8th
Tacoma, WA 98405-0000
(253) 571-2645

The Vancouver Schools of Arts and Academics
3101 Main Street
Vancouver, WA 98663
(360) 313-4600
www.vansd.org/vocweb/mfact/arts.html

Southwest

Luz Academy of Tucson
2797 N. Introspect Drive
Tucson, AZ 85745
(520) 882-6216
www.luzacademy.com

Middle College High School at El Centro Community College
Main and Lamar Streets
Dallas, TX 75202
(214) 860-2356

Rehoboth Christian School
P.O. Box 41
Rehoboth, NM 87322
(505) 863-4412
www.rcsnm.org

West

East Palo Alto High School
475 Pope Street
Menlo Park, CA
(650) 329-2811

Foshay Learning Center
3751 South Harvard Boulevard
Los Angeles, CA 90018
(323) 735-0241
www.foshay.k12.ca.us

New Tech High
920 Yount Street
Napa, CA 94559
(707) 259-8557
www.newtechhigh.com

Preuss School
9500 Gilman Drive, #0536
La Jolla, CA
(858) 658-7400
preuss.ucsd.edu/

Research on
Small High Schools

Allen, L.,w with Almeida, C., & Steinberg, A. (2001, August). Wall to wall: Implementing small learning communities in five Boston high schools. *LAB Working Paper No. 3*. Providence, RI: Northeast and Islands Regional Educational Laboratory, a program of The Education Alliance at Brown University. www.lab.brown.edu/public/pubs/LABWorkPaper/Wall2Wall.pdf

Ancess, J., & Ort, S. W. (1999, March). *How the coalition campus schools have re-imagined high school: Seven years later.* New York: National Center for Restructuring Education, Schools and Teaching, Teachers College, Columbia University. www.tc.columbia.edu/~ncrest/aera_ancess.pdf

Boss, S. (2000, Winter). Big lessons on a small scale. *Northwest Education Magazine, 6* (2). www.nwrel.org/nwedu/winter_00/1.html

Boyer, E. (1983). *High school: A report on secondary education in America.* New York: Harper & Row.

Clinchy, E., ed. (2000). *Creating new schools: how small schools are changing American education.* New York: Teachers College Press, Columbia University.

Cotton, K. (2001, December). *New small learning communities: Findings from recent literature.* Portland, OR: Northwest Regional Educational Laboratory. www.nwrel.org/scpd/sirs/nslc.pdf

Cushman, K. (1999, November). How small schools increase student learning (and what large schools can do about it). *Principal, 79* (2), 20–22. www.naesp.org/comm/p1199b.htm

Goodlad, J. (1984). *A place called school: Promise for the future.* New York: McGraw-Hill.

Gregory, T. (1992). Small is too big: Achieving a critical anti-mass in the high school. In *Source book on school and district size, cost, and quality* (pp. 1–31). Minneapolis: Minnesota University, Hubert H. Humphrey Institute of Public Affairs; Oak Book, IL: North Central Regional Laboratory. www.gatesfoundation.org/NR/downloads/ed/evaluation/smallistoobig.pdf

———. (2000, December). *School reform and the no-man's-land of high school size*. Seattle, WA: Center on Reinventing Public Education. www.gatesfoundation.org/education/resources-research/schoolreformtgregory.pdf

———. (2001). Breaking up large high schools: Five common (and understandable) errors of execution. *ERIC Digest*. ERIC Clearinghouse on Rural Education and Small Schools. www.ael.org/eric/digests/edorco1-6.htm

Howley, C., Strange, M., & Bickel, R. (2000, December). Research about school size and school performance in impoverished communities. *ERIC Digest*. ERIC Clearinghouse on Rural Education and Small Schools. EDO-RC-00-10. www.ael.org/eric/digests/edorco010.htm

Howley, C., & Bickel, R. (2000). *School size, poverty, and student achievement*. The Rural School and Community Trust. www.ruraledu.org/matthew.html

Marsh, D., & Codding, J. (1998). *The new American high school*. Thousand Oaks, CA: Corwin Press.

McAndrews, T., & Anderson, W. (2002, January). *Schools within schools*. ERIC Digest 154. Clearinghouse on Educational Management. ED-99-Co-0011. eric.uoregon.edu/publications/digests/digest154.html

McPartland, J., Jordan, W., Letgers, N., & Balfanz, R. (1997, October). Finding safety in small numbers. *Educational*

Leadership, 55 (2), 14–17. www.ascd.org/readingroom/
edlead/9710/mcpartland.html

Meier, Deborah. (1995). *The power of their ideas: Lessons for
America from a small school in Harlem*. Boston: Beacon Press.

———. (1996.) The big benefits of smallness. *Educational
Leadership*, 54 (1), 12–15. www.ascd.org/readingroom/
edlead/9609/meier.html

———. (2002). *In schools we trust: Creating communities of
learning in an era of testing and standardization*. Boston:
Beacon Press.

Mitchell, S. (2000, Summer). Jack and the giant school.
The New Rules, 2 (1). www.newrules.org/journal/
nrsumooschools.htm

Nathan, J., & Febey, K. (2001). *Smaller, safer, saner, successful schools*. Washington, DC: National Clearinghouse
for Educational Facilities and Minneapolis: The Center for School Change, Humphrey Institute of the
University of Minnesota. www.edfacilities.org/pubs/
saneschools.pdf

Raywid, M. A. (1996). Downsizing schools in big cities
ERIC Digest. ERIC Clearinghouse on Urban Education.
EDO-UD-96-1. www.ael.org/eric/digests/edoud961.htm

———. (1997, December; 1998, January). Small schools: A reform that works. *Educational Leadership, 55* (4), 34–39. www.ascd.org/readingroom/edlead/9712/raywid.html

Roellke, C. (1996). Curriculum adequacy and quality in high schools enrolling fewer than 400 pupils (9–12). *ERIC Digest.* ERIC Clearinghouse on Rural Education and Small Schools. EDO-RC-96-7. www.ael.org/eric/digests/edorc967.htm

Sizer, T. R. (1984). *Horace's compromise: The dilemma of the American high school.* Boston: Houghton Mifflin.

———. (1992). *Horace's school: Redesigning the American high school.* Boston: Houghton Mifflin.

———. (1996). *Horace's hope: What works for the American high school.* Boston: Houghton Mifflin.

U.S. Department of Education, Office of Elementary and Secondary Education and Office of Vocational and Adult Education. (2001, November). *An overview of smaller learning communities in high schools.* Washington, DC: Author. www.ed.gov/offices/OESE/SLCP/slchighschools_research_09_01.doc

What Kids Can Do. *A close look at student work in small schools: Work portfolios.* www.whatkidscando.org/smallschools/intro.html

Winokur, M. (2001, June). *Policy brief: Relationship between high school size and educational outcomes.* Colorado State University: Research and Development Center for the Advancement of Student Learning. www.colostate.edu/depts/r-dcenter/policybriefs.html

Acknowledgments

I was thrilled when Tom Vander Ark, the thoughtful director of the education program at the Bill & Melinda Gates
Foundation, gave me a chance to write about one of the
most pressing challenges in American education today—
the need to overhaul the nation's public high schools. The
nation has never sought to educate more than a fraction of
its high school students to high levels. But now that the
world of work has changed so profoundly it must, if today's
students are to achieve the standard of living that their parents and grandparents acquired with far less education.

The schools that I describe in this book possess qualities
that are the key building blocks of the new kind of high
school that we need to address this daunting challenge. The

schools were gracious hosts during my visits, permitting me to observe and interview students, teachers, parents, and others freely. I shared early drafts of the profiles of each school with the head of the school as a way of ensuring that my profiles were factually accurate. The schools, however, did not exercise editorial control.

Nor did the Bill & Melinda Gates Foundation. Tom Vander Ark asked me to tell the stories of schools that collectively represent a new model of the American public high school, one capable of educating a wide range of students to high levels in academic subjects. He identified a number of schools that he and his colleagues sensed had features to contribute to the new American high school. I studied these schools and selected several to write about in depth. The characterizations of the schools in this book are mine alone.

The Gates staff, however, was supportive at every turn. David Ferrero, the foundation's education research director, provided valuable comments on early drafts. And Peter Bloch Garcia, David's assistant, was always happy to lend his help when I needed it.

Andy Hrycyna, my editor at Beacon Press, was a pleasure to work with. Not surprisingly, given his talents, he found many ways to strengthen the book. Claire Hollywood served as an able and enterprising research assistant. Copyeditor Doug Colglazier proffered a keen eye and a deft touch.

Marc Tucker was generous to give me a home at the

National Center on Education and the Economy midway through the project. Marc has long been an astute observer of the American high school experience, and his insights and those of NCEE colleague Judy Codding have been invaluable to me.

The most important things there are to learn about education and educating, though, I've learned from my wife, Ann, and my children, Matthew and Caroline. I have been very lucky to have such wonderful teachers.